T0153540

MISS
GOD

MISS
GOD

Claus Mikosch

Illustrations by Kate Chesterton

AMMONITE
PRESS

Contents

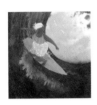

For Charlotte and Rocío

Prologue

livia sat in front of her empty plate, staring through the window. Her dreamy gaze followed a white cloud drifting peacefully across the sky. Where is it heading to, she wondered, and could it perhaps take me for a little ride? It must be wonderful to be able to watch the world from above for a while, far from the noise and the daily worries and yet close enough to observe life. For a moment she could hear the wind and the swooshing of the nearby sea; in her mind's eye, she could see the waves dancing with the sunlight and rolling slowly towards the shore. A few seagulls appeared and she watched them gently glide through the air. Everything seemed so easy, so perfect and so blissfully harmonious.

Then suddenly – screaming. Yanked out of her peaceful daydream Olivia glanced to her left, where her mother was wildly waving a fork in her hand while shouting at Olivia's father, who was sitting to her right with his arms crossed. Her parents' fights had become a regular part of their lunches. Usually they were about their lack of money or time, or both. They also argued about the news or the house, at times even about the weather. There was always something. Sometimes her mother hurled angry words through the air, other times her father recited never-ending monologues full of blame. And it always resulted in a sulky silence on both sides and loud sobbing; there was rarely a happy end. Olivia didn't understand why they couldn't get along, nor did she know why she always ended up in the middle, having to listen to all the drama.

'Can I go for a walk with Albert?' she asked her mother, who had at last put her fork down.

'Ask your father,' was the angry reply.

Olivia turned to the other side of the table.

'Dad, can I go for a walk with Albert?'

'Sure, sweetheart,' he said, while pouring himself another glass of wine to drown his sorrows.

Olivia got up, took her plate into the kitchen and left the small holiday apartment accompanied by Albert, her faithful Jack Russell terrier. She closed the door behind her and took a deep breath. It wasn't easy to be the daughter of unhappy parents.

Ten minutes later she had reached the beach and was strolling along the shore. Albert chased past her, playfully greeting the approaching waves. Olivia wore a blue hoodie, a short olive-green skirt and dark-red leggings. Her brown hair was arranged into two braids and she walked over the soft sand with bare feet. It was a Sunday in September. Olivia was eleven years old.

Together with her parents, she lived in a big town, a two-hour drive away. They came to the coast three to four times a year to spend a weekend in the nice little village, which consisted of eighty-five houses and a red lighthouse. According to Olivia's father, these trips were all about leaving the stress behind for a few days but unfortunately her parents always took the stress with them. Olivia had to find her own peace.

Sometimes she wondered whether they were really her parents because, as much as she tried, she could only find a few things she had in common with them. Maybe she had been mixed up with someone else's child at birth? And now it was her who had to pay for the mistake of the hospital staff. Luckily she always had an excuse to escape from the two quarrel addicts thanks to her dog. And was there a better place to find peace than by the sea? Over the years it had become an irreplaceable friend away from home.

The summer season had ended a few weeks earlier so the beach was almost empty. Only a few other dog owners were out and occasionally she passed a lone fisherman. Olivia set one foot in front of the other and enjoyed the calmness of nature surrounding her. She collected some shells and watched Albert continuing to pace along the shore with great joy when, suddenly, he ran to the top of the beach and disappeared behind a small sand dune. She waited, but after a few minutes he still hadn't returned. She called his name a few times and whistled with her fingers. Her uncle had shown her how to do this, a year ago, just a few months before he died.

'Albert!' she tried again, but there was no sign of the little terrier.

Olivia had no choice but to go and look for him. She climbed the little hill and, when she got to the top, was surprised to see a wooden hut right behind the sand dune. Over the years she had walked hundreds of kilometres along the same beach, but she had never noticed the hut before.

'Albert!' she shouted, and then she finally spotted his wagging tail. He was sitting happily in front of a wooden bench on the hut's veranda and was letting himself be petted by an old woman with white, curly hair. Olivia whistled vigorously, but Albert ignored her.

'That's strange,' she thought, 'normally he comes straight away when I'm nearby.' She wanted to shout again but fell silent when a sudden gust of wind swept over the dune. The wind caught a piece of paper that was lying next to the woman and carried it away. Instinctively, Olivia ran after the flying sheet, finally catching it after three attempts. Slowly she returned to the hut, and while walking back took a closer look at the piece of paper she was holding in her hand. At the top, something was written in old-fashioned letters. Olivia had to stop for a moment to decipher the writing: 'The New Ten Commandments'. The rest of the page was empty.

She stepped on to the veranda, greeted the woman and handed her the piece of paper.

'Thank you for fetching that for me, that's very kind of you.'

Olivia smiled politely, then turned to her dog with a serious tone.

'Albert, what's the matter? Why don't you come when I call you?'

The little terrier stared at her with big puppy eyes, but he didn't leave his spot. Only now did the woman stop stroking him. She put the piece of paper next to her on the bench and placed a cup on it so that it couldn't fly away again.

'That's an unusual name for a dog.'

Olivia shrugged her shoulders.

'It was my grandfather's name.'

'I see.'

The old woman gave her a compassionate smile. She wore a long, light-blue dress with a floral pattern and her white hair reached just below her ears. Olivia guessed she was at least seventy.

'Do you live here?' Olivia asked.

'Yes.'

'How long have you lived here?'

'For a few months.'

'And who else lives here?'

'Nobody. After all, it's just a small hut. And besides, I enjoy being alone.'

Olivia wasn't sure what to make of her. She seemed nice and friendly, but something was odd about her. It was probably best to leave.

'Come on Albert, we need to go.'

But Albert showed no intention of leaving.

'Why don't you sit down for a bit?' the woman said and pointed to an inviting rocking chair next to the bench. 'I could make you a hot chocolate, if you want. As a thank you for helping me.'

Olivia looked at Albert, whose tail drummed the wooden floor with excitement. She thought for a moment. A hot chocolate wouldn't actually be too bad. And for some reason she was curious to learn more about the old woman.

'Okay then.'

She sat down on the chair and the woman disappeared inside the hut to make the promised drink. Olivia thought of her mother, who always told her never to accept invitations from strangers. But it was just an old woman, what harm could she do?

Her eyes caught the piece of paper, trapped under the cup and lightly fluttering in the wind. She read the mysterious headline once more. Only recently she'd had to memorize the Ten Commandments in her religious education class at school. In fact, that was the second time she'd had to learn them, because when she was nine years old she'd had to memorize them for her communion. It was a complete waste of time! They were written in such a weird language and hardly anyone kept to the commandments anyway. Everywhere there were divorces, wars and lies, and, despite the Sabbath command, she still had to do homework on Sundays. They were a joke, these commandments! She had only endured the communion to please her grandmother – and because of the fancy bicycle she'd been given as a present.

'Here's your hot chocolate,' the woman said as she stepped through the door holding a bright-yellow cup.

'Thanks!'

The woman sat down on the bench again and Albert immediately sat back into stroking position. Olivia stirred her hot chocolate and gently rocked on her chair. For a few moments, only the wind and the surf were to be heard.

After a little while, Olivia asked, 'Why does it say "The New Ten Commandments" on the paper?'

The woman took her eyes off Albert, looked at the girl and smiled with a hint of sadness.

'Because unfortunately humans haven't properly understood the old commandments. So, I'm trying to write new ones.'

'Why?' the girl wondered.

'Because I want to help the humans.'

Olivia looked startled.

'What do you mean, "the humans"?'

The woman hesitated and looked deeply into her visitor's eyes for a long time. Then she let out a sigh.

'I'm God.'

Olivia almost dropped the cup. She barely managed to keep her balance and avoid a bigger accident.

'What did you say?' She must have misunderstood the old woman.

'I'm God.'

'You're who?'

'God,' the woman repeated in a calm tone, as if it were totally normal to say something like that.

Olivia started to laugh.

'But God is a man.'

Now the woman also laughed. But only for a short moment.

'Is he?' she challenged her.

Olivia stopped laughing too and stared at her.

'You seriously want to tell me you're God?'

A queasy feeling rose inside her. What if she was sitting here with a complete lunatic? She regretted having accepted the offer of the hot chocolate. Now what?

'It's quite interesting,' the woman said as she stirred her own drink. 'One would think that if a stranger tells you she's God, that you would first doubt whether that person really is God. Instead, you doubt that God could be a woman.'

Olivia looked at her, speechless.

'Sure, God is usually referred to as "He",' the old woman continued. 'But it wasn't me who decided that. Back then, when the Bible was written and people tried to describe me more accurately, the men made all the important decisions. Of course they saw a man in me, because a woman could not possibly be the mighty ruler of the world. And sadly, today it's still more or less the same.'

She took a long sip of her drink.

'At the end of the day, I don't care if people see me as a man or a woman. Because, in reality, I am both. How else could it be?'

Olivia shook her head in disbelief. Either she was dreaming, or someone was trying to fool her. It was time to wake up. Or to leave.

'I think I have to go home.'

'But you haven't finished your hot chocolate yet.'

'Never mind.'

Olivia put the cup on the floor and was about to get out of the chair when the woman carefully placed her hand on Olivia's knee. It was a warm hand, calm and caring.

'Are you scared of me?'

Olivia didn't move.

'Or do you think that I'm crazy?'

'A little bit, yes,' she admitted.

'I understand that. After all, you don't meet God every day.'

The woman winked at her and took her hand back. Olivia should have jumped up and run away but something stopped her. Something deep inside her. Besides, she liked what the old woman had said. Indeed, why shouldn't God be a woman? It certainly didn't sound like a mad idea. And then there was Albert, of course, who was still stuck to the stranger's leg. Nobody had a better understanding of human nature than the little terrier.

Olivia decided to trust the old woman.

'Alright, I will finish my hot chocolate. But I don't really believe that you're God.'

'You don't have to,' said the woman. She paused for a moment. 'What about a little game?'

'What kind of game?' Olivia replied, sceptically.

'A bit like role play. Try to imagine that I am really God. It would be a great opportunity for you: you can personally speak to the famous creator of the world!'

Olivia still felt sceptical, but since she had decided to trust the woman, she agreed to the game and nodded.

'Good. So, what would you ask God?'

'I would ...'

She stopped mid-sentence and thought about it. What would she want to know from God? The image of her dying uncle came to her mind. For many months he had fought against cancer and had suffered incredible agony. And on television she often saw terrible images of war – children her own age, without legs, without parents, without hope. And the poor people on the street who have nothing to eat. To all of that she would like to get an answer.

'Why is there so much suffering in the world?'

Miss God sat motionless for a moment, then she started to nod.

'Yes, that's a very good question ...'

'You don't know the answer? But if you are God you must know this. So why don't you change anything?'

'If only it were that easy,' the old woman replied, sounding dejected. 'You humans always think that I'm responsible for every one of you and that I can direct your life as I wish. Neither is true, though. I am mother and father, yes, but neither ruler nor puppet master nor anyone else who takes away the control over your own life.'

'Does this mean you can't punish anyone either? What about hell?'

This made Miss God laugh heartily.

'Heaven and hell, with little angels and devils, what a funny idea that was! But unfortunately, this concept causes terrible fear and is not true at all. I can't punish anyone, no.'

'Can you save someone?'

The old woman stalled for a few moments, taking a sip from her cup.

'Not directly. But I can transmit messages to those who listen. I can tell them how life could be better and happier for everyone.'

'You mean priests and such.'

'Sometimes priests, yes. But it can be anyone.'

'Was Moses such a person?'

'Yes, and Jesus too. And Buddha and Mohammed and Krishna. Right now, you are.'

Olivia looked at her, puzzled.

'What do you mean by that?'

They studied each other in silence. Even the wind had stopped completely and seemed to listen curiously. Then Miss God smiled. It was an honest, motherly smile.

'I'm just talking to you. That's all.'

Olivia didn't really know what was happening to her. The situation she was in did seem like a game, like a made-up story. Yet at the same time it was so bizarre it almost had to be true.

'Do you want to keep playing for a bit? Because I could really do with some help.'

'You want me to help you? With what?'

'With the Ten Commandments.' Miss God started patting Albert again. 'What do you think of them?'

Olivia wasn't sure how to answer.

'Do you want to know the truth?' Olivia asked.

'Of course. You can say whatever you want.'

'Alright,' she said. 'I think they're totally stupid.'

Miss God grinned.

'And why?'

'Because they only talk about what we mustn't do. You should have called them "The Ten Prohibitions". They're all "you shouldn't do this and you shouldn't do that". When my parents talk to me that way I don't even listen properly!'

Miss God was surprised.

'I have to admit I hadn't thought of it that way. But you're absolutely right: prohibitions aren't very encouraging. See, you've already helped me!'

Olivia felt flattered. The game wasn't that bad after all.

'In my defence though,' said the old woman, 'I must add that I neither mentioned commandments nor prohibitions when I spoke to Moses. They were simply some suggestions. Moses had understood this but later, when his words were written down, other people made quite a lot of changes. You'll find there are many other things in the Bible that have nothing to do with me.' She thought for a moment. 'For example, at one point it says that women should be silent in the communities, that they're not allowed to talk and that they should be submissive instead. Do you really think I would say something like that?'

Miss God looked at Olivia questioningly. The girl shook her head.

'But if you write new commandments now, it could happen again, someone could change something,' Olivia said. 'And in the end most people don't stick to the commandments anyway. Not even people who go to church every week.'

Miss God let out another long sigh.

'I wish I could disagree with you.' Her shoulders dropped. 'It's really sad, isn't it? You give them some well-meant advice and what do they do? They fight and argue and say terrible things about each other. They do exactly the opposite of what the commandments say.'

This time it was Olivia who smiled compassionately. It was a moment she would probably tell her grandchildren about: the time God sat in front of her wondering what the world had come to.

'Yet still, it's worth a try,' the old woman said, unwilling to give up. 'Perhaps the commandments will reach more people if I phrase them differently. They're not all bad, they're just expressed in an unfavourable manner. Just like in the Bible, where you find many useful things too.'

'So why don't you write a new Bible?'

'I already thought of that too, but on the one hand it's far too much work, and on the other people read less and less nowadays.'

Olivia nodded in agreement.

'Especially big books, nobody has time for them anymore.'

Another gust of wind swept over the veranda. This time Miss God managed to grab the piece of paper before it could fly away.

'So, what do you think? Are you going to help me a bit more? I would love to know what you think about each commandment.'

Olivia hesitated and turned to Albert. He had made himself comfortable on a colourful, round carpet on the wooden floor. Her parents were probably still busy blaming each other for their own dissatisfaction. Or they were already fast asleep, just like after every big fight. Either way, she wouldn't miss anything if she stayed with the old woman for a while longer. And yes, the situation was crazy and strange, but she was enjoying this little role-playing game. There was still a lot she could ask Miss God.

For example, why did she have to learn so many useless things at school? Why is the boy next door blind, and why don't her parents get along? Why is she here, on Earth, in this body? What happens after death? And how did God become God?

She decided to keep playing.

'Can I have some more hot chocolate?'

1
Life

lright, number one,' said the old woman after topping up Olivia's cup. 'The Bible says ...'

'"I am the Lord, your God",' Olivia cut in. '"Thou shalt have no other gods before me".'

Miss God raised her eyebrows, seemingly impressed.

'Very good.'

She leaned forwards and picked up a notepad and pen from under the bench. She thought for a moment.

'We can eliminate the Lord straight away.'

Both grinned. Then the old woman wrote down the first sentence: I am your God.

'Okay?'

Olivia slowly pulled her shoulders towards her ears. She wasn't really convinced.

'But who is God?'

The woman looked at her in surprise.

'I'm sitting right in front of you, aren't I?' she laughed.

Olivia rolled her eyes.

'Fine. But what if I read this and you're not sitting in front of me, and you've never sat in front of me before?'

Silence.

'The commandments also say that you shouldn't create any image of God. So how am I supposed to imagine God? Who is it supposed to be?' asked Olivia.

'Perhaps it's just an idea.'

'An idea?'

Olivia didn't really know what the old woman meant by that.

'Yes, an idea. A concept invented by humans to describe something that no one can describe.'

Once more, the old woman spoke about humans as if she herself wasn't one of them. It was really strange.

'Something that is bigger than the human being because humans tend to feel rather small. And compared to the whole universe they are indeed nothing more than tiny ants. So it's helpful to feel that you belong to a greater entity. Besides, I think the idea of God can help to give meaning to life.'

While Olivia was still pondering the human ant hill, Miss God took a sip from her cup.

'So how have you imagined God so far?' she asked.

Olivia shook her head.

'I don't know,' she said. 'Definitely always as a man.' She gave the old woman an apologetic look. 'When I was younger, I used to think that He was some kind of king in heaven.'

Miss God had to laugh.

'And today?'

Olivia hesitated. She didn't really have a clear idea.

'I probably wouldn't think of God as a person anymore. More like ...'

She stared to her right, in the direction of the sand dune. She thought long and hard, but nothing came to mind.

'Maybe it's easier if you don't ask yourself who God is, but what God is?' the old woman suggested.

Olivia continued to stare straight ahead. A few new clouds had gathered in the sky.

'God could be like the sun,' she said after a while.

'Yes, there's certainly something divine about the sun,' the woman agreed. 'In the past, thousands of years ago, many people worshipped the sun. Because it's the sun that gives light and warmth and therefore also life.'

But Olivia had already stopped listening.

'Maybe God is love,' she thought out loud.

'Oh, love. I like that,' said Miss God. She grabbed the pen and wrote down the word 'love'.

There was silence for another moment. Olivia took her eyes from the sky and turned back to her hostess.

'And what about the other gods?'

'What do you mean?'

'In the first commandment it says you shouldn't have any other gods.'

Olivia was confused. If God is love, how can there be any other gods?

'Again, it was humans who came up with the various gods. I don't really understand it either.' Miss God shifted around on her bench restlessly. 'The Bible even says that I'm a jealous God and that I will punish those who are not faithful to me. Such nonsense!'

'So, you're not jealous?'

'No, of course not. Who should I be jealous of? Myself?' She made a questioning gesture with her hands and shook her head. 'There is only one God and that's me,' she added self-assuredly.

Olivia carefully smiled at her. The old woman played her role really well. Almost a little too well.

'Have you already talked about the different religions at school?'

Olivia nodded.

'I'm not against them,' Miss God continued. 'But unfortunately most people confuse something very important.'

She skipped to an empty page in her little notepad and drew a cross so that Olivia could see it.

'On the horizontal axis are the religions.' She drew a few circles on the line. 'There are many different groups, small and big ones, where people who worship God in the same way come together. A bit like the fans of a sports club: people sing, celebrate and mourn together.' For a moment she paused. 'Hence religion is something that connects people.'

Olivia followed attentively.

'And then there's the vertical axis. That's faith.'

Miss God drew a happy face at the bottom of the vertical line and at the top she wrote ME in capital letters.

'Faith is a direct connection between a person and God.'

She began to draw more vertical lines and next to the ME she added two long arms, stretching out to the right and left.

'There are as many vertical lines as there are people and all lead to the same God. Only the way in which each person imagines God differs.'

Olivia looked at the drawing.

'It's really quite simple,' the old woman said after a brief pause. 'Some imagine a river, others a lake and again others the ocean. But in the end, everybody imagines water.'

'That would mean that all religions are connected with each other, right?'

'Yes.'

'And one isn't better than the other?'

Miss God shook her head.

'All religions say many good and true things. However, they all say a lot of stupid things too.'

Now it was Olivia who had to laugh. It was a likeable God sitting there in front of her.

'Whenever I spoke to Jesus, Buddha, Mohammed and Moses,' the old woman continued, 'I told them all more or less the same thing. We talked about faith, about life, love and happiness. Only much later, these words were converted into religions. And then over time every religion made up their own story.'

'But it doesn't matter if there are different stories,' Olivia said.

'No, it doesn't. But the problem is that everyone thinks only their story is true. And then they argue about who is right.'

Indeed, Olivia thought. Not only in the case of her parents but in general, there was far too much fighting in the world. She looked at the drawing.

'So, I can believe in God without belonging to a religion,' she concluded.

Miss God nodded and smiled at her.

'Just like you, right now, everyone can have a personal relationship with me. Even more so, everyone can imagine God as they wish. As an old man with a long grey beard, a golden sun, love, an elephant or a tree. As long as your faith helps you to be happy and peaceful, it doesn't matter what you believe in.'

Olivia wondered whether there are really people who worship an elephant or a tree, at least she couldn't exclude the possibility. And if such people exist, they probably also ask themselves if there are really people who worship an old man with a grey beard!

'If it makes someone happy to go to church and read thick holy books,' the old woman said, 'then that's wonderful. But you don't need a church nor a holy book to meet God. Just look around you!'

She pointed to the bright-blue sky and to the sea glistening between the sand dunes. A fresh breeze touched their faces and, in the distance, they could hear seabirds calling.

'I, for one, prefer to talk out here rather than inside a dark building,' Miss God stated.

Olivia smiled in agreement. She also preferred to sit on a rocking chair by the beach than on a hard, wooden bench in front of an altar. And if God really is about light and sun and loving warmth, then all church services should take place outdoors.

She looked at the old woman, who had started to stroke Albert again. Olivia liked what she had to say and for the first time she saw nothing crazy in her. On the contrary, if she were really God, surely she would be a good God.

'So, what should we write for the first commandment?' the old woman asked.

Olivia shrugged her shoulders.

'Definitely something that doesn't sound sad or scary.'

She thought of her grandmother, who was her Dad's mother and the only one of her grandparents who was still alive. Olivia loved her dearly but there was one thing she didn't understand.

'Everyone can imagine God as they wish. As an old man with a long grey beard, a golden sun, love, an elephant or a tree. As long as your faith helps you to be happy and peaceful, it doesn't matter what you believe in.'

'When my grandmother is reminiscing about my grandfather, she sometimes says that he used to be a God-fearing man. That's terrible! Why should anyone be scared of God?'

The old woman let out another long sigh.

'If there are commandments, they should at least be nice,' Olivia continued. 'It would be much better if they caused joy instead of fear.'

Miss God nodded silently. Her face revealed that she felt slightly guilty about people being afraid of her. She had never used a word like God-fearing herself but perhaps she should have tried to correct this misunderstanding a long time ago. She was clearly uncomfortable about having to be reminded of it now, and by an eleven-year-old girl no less.

'Something that causes joy,' she repeated Olivia's suggestion. She thought for a moment and recapped.

'Until now it said, "I am the Lord, your God. Thou shalt have no other gods beside me". We've already got rid of the Lord, and we better take out the other gods too. That leaves us with God. And love.'

Olivia considered the two words and rubbed her nose, which was a little too big for her liking.

'What about the people who don't believe in God?' she said after a short pause. 'Maybe we better get rid of God too.'

She thought of her Dad, who was a stubborn atheist. And of the blind boy who lived next door and had never believed in God but hated him all the same.

'You're right,' Miss God replied. 'They wouldn't feel addressed at all. Despite being connected to me even without faith.'

For a while they both sat in silence, drank from their cups and pondered the possibilities.

'Which word could be used instead of God?' the old woman mumbled to herself. 'It should be something that appeals to everyone. All religions, atheists, children, adults, the healthy, the sick, the rich and the poor.'

Olivia rubbed her nose again. She did that often when she needed ideas.

Meanwhile, Miss God tapped her pen against the notepad.

'Love and ...'

The second word didn't want to appear.

'How would you describe yourself?' Olivia asked. 'With one word only.'

Miss God stopped tapping her pen and paused.

'Everything,' she finally said.

'Everything?'

Miss God nodded.

'Everything is a part of me. In a sense we are all God: you, me, your parents and friends, Albert, the sand, the sun, the waves and the wind. Together we shape life.'

'Life ...' Olivia repeated.

The old woman froze for a moment, then a beaming smile began to spread across her face.

'Life!' she shouted. 'I am life, that's exactly what it is!'

Olivia grinned, satisfied.

'So, we have love and life,' Miss God concluded. 'Life and love, to love and to live.'

And suddenly they both knew what the first commandment would be.

'To love life,' they said together.

Albert happily wagged his tail and the wind signalled its approval with a soft breeze.

They had taken the first step.

2
Respect

‘Nine to go,’ said Miss God. She was about to continue with the second commandment when Olivia had a different thought.

‘Can you tell me why there are ten commandments?’

The old woman gave her a questioning look.

‘Why not five? Or three? Or why not stop at the first one: "Love life". You don't need to know more.’

Miss God's smile showed that she liked that idea.

‘Indeed, you don't really need to know more. If you always remember to love life, only good things can come about every time you make a decision.’ She hesitated. ‘But I think most people have got used to the number ten. If suddenly there was only one commandment, many would probably assume it has nothing to do with God. Besides, I think that people can do with a few more rules.’

‘Rules?’

Another one of those words Olivia didn't like at all.

‘Rules, commandments, suggestions – you can call them what you like. Something that provides guidance. Something you can lean on in times of uncertainty.’ The old woman looked at Albert, who had risen from the carpet and was stretching. ‘Let's see how far we get. If it gets too late or if we get tired, we can stop.’

Olivia agreed with a short nod. Then she looked at her dog, who slowly came towards her with his tongue hanging out. She began to shake her head and made a resentful face.

‘Now that you want something from me you come crawling over. That's not nice, Albert!’ she scolded him. Then she turned to Miss God. ‘Could I get some water for him?’

‘Sure!’ she said straight away, getting up and going inside.

Olivia gave the little terrier another stern look before swinging herself back into the rocking chair and ignoring him. While rocking back and forth, she wondered what her best friend would say if she told her about her encounter with Miss God. Surely she'd laugh at her, but of course it's easy to make fun of someone if you haven't experienced the situation yourself. The old woman was so convincing in her role Olivia had to constantly remind herself that it was just a game. She tried to keep a clear head but the longer the conversation lasted, the thinner the line between reality and fantasy became. Often she had the feeling that she really was sitting in front of God. And if it really was God then there was one thing she definitely had to find out: of all people, why was it her who had met God? Why not her best friend, her mother or her father?

She heard the rattling of some pots and plates from inside the hut. Shortly afterwards the old woman came back with a bowl of water and placed it on the floor next to Albert, who immediately began to slurp greedily.

'Alright, the second commandment,' she said, ready for action.

Olivia let go of her thoughts about the reason for this encounter and returned to the commandments.

'"Thou shalt not take the name of the Lord thy God in vain",' she quoted as if she had learned the words only the previous day.

Miss God tapped her pen against the notepad again, contemplating.

'If we take out the Lord, just like in the first commandment, and replace him with life, we'd have ...' She was looking for a good phrase. 'Thou shalt not take life in vain?'

Olivia wrinkled her nose.

'Too complicated. And too negative.'

'You're right.'

They continued to consider other options while Albert got comfortable on his carpet again.

'What exactly do you mean by this commandment?' Olivia wondered.

'I actually didn't say it like this,' Miss God replied.

'So how did you say it?'

'I'm not sure. It was a long time ago,' she justified herself.

Olivia found it reassuring that even God seemed to have a few memory problems.

'And you? What do you think it means?' the old woman wanted to know.

'That you shouldn't talk bad about God. And our priest also used to say that you shouldn't swear. But I don't understand this, why is it important? What does swearing have to do with God?'

The woman smiled.

'Don't worry, it's not forbidden to swear. Sometimes swearing can actually help to vent your anger. Or to better describe a strong feeling. For example, when you say that you are angry or happy.'

She paused and took a deep breath before continuing in a more serious tone.

'However, people underestimate the power of language. If you swear a lot and use ugly words, it's as if you're constantly spitting fire. Those around you might feel bothered or even attacked. And in the long run the fire can leave its mark on you too. It's like your soul is getting burned.'

Olivia gulped. A burnt soul – that didn't sound very nice.

'Like with smoking when the lungs turn black,' she tried a comparison.

'Yes, a bit like that. Lots of swearing is not as harmful as smoking but it can still make you sick. Not the lungs, but the heart. Happy people don't swear much, that's for sure.'

Olivia thought of her parents and hoped they weren't suffering too badly. They were always swearing like hell.

'But there's something that I find much worse than a few unnecessary swear words,' Miss God said after a short silence. 'It's the wars people keep fighting in my name. Unfortunately, there are no exceptions, all religions are guilty! It's outrageous: they insist it was me who gave them the order to go to war.' Anger rose in the old woman. 'Trust me, if I could punish them, I wouldn't hesitate for a second!'

Olivia would have never imagined seeing God so furious. But she felt sympathy nonetheless.

'Why do wars actually exist?' she wanted to know. 'Couldn't you have created a world without wars?'

'That's what I did,' Miss God said in frustration. 'There's enough food and space for everyone and yet still most people feel they don't have enough. They think someone could take something away from them, be it their food, their land or their faith. But that's totally absurd!'

Miss God reached for her cup and took a sip to calm herself down. In the meantime, Olivia stared into her own hot chocolate and thought of the breaks in the schoolyard where she always witnessed fights of all kinds. The boys wanted to be the strongest and the girls the most beautiful.

'Maybe wars have to do with wanting to win,' she finally said.

'Yes, I think you're right,' the old woman replied. 'At the end of the day it's all about power games. To gain new power or to defend the power you already have. And to avoid losing at all cost! During a competition – in sports or at school – it might be entertaining and appropriate that you want to win. But when people get hurt, the way they do in wars, it's not a game anymore.'

Olivia nodded, lost in thought. Luckily, she had never experienced war herself but the dreadful images on television were enough to make her biggest wish be for peace. She wondered why all these conflicts existed.

'And why do people want to have power?'

'It gives them a feeling of security. Because the truth is that, deep inside, they are terribly afraid. They fear poverty, loneliness and, worst of all, death. Power gives them the illusion that they can control those fears.' Miss God sighed. 'But of course, it doesn't work like that. The fears stay alive and each time the people's power is threatened they start to lash out wildly. Hence all the quarrels and wars.'

They both looked at the ground, then into each other's eyes with great sadness.

'You know,' the old woman continued, 'faith can help you with all those fears. It gives you hope when you're poor, it provides company when you feel lonely and it fills you with trust when the unknown of death nears.

*Miss God reached for her cup
and took a sip to calm herself
down. In the meantime, Olivia
stared into her own hot chocolate
and thought of the breaks in the
schoolyard where she always
witnessed fights of all kinds.*

And that's exactly why people are so sensitive when it comes to their faith. Because faith is the only true remedy for their greatest fears.'

Olivia understood what the woman was saying but she was still unsure why wars had to happen. Especially wars because of God, that didn't make any sense whatsoever.

'You've explained that faith is the direct connection between a person and God. So how should it be possible that anyone can take away my faith?'

The old woman shrugged her shoulders.

'As I've said, it's totally absurd.'

She shook her head, staring past her visitor and towards the sea.

'I really don't understand why you humans are so afraid of each other. Just because someone looks, thinks or believes differently, you feel threatened straight away. Why aren't you happy about the diversity that exists? If everyone was the same, you wouldn't like that either.' She looked at Olivia. 'Imagine all the trees in the world were pine trees. How boring would that be!'

She shook her head again, and let her eyes drift back to the horizon.

'Why can't you simply be nice to each other?' she quietly wondered to herself.

Olivia kept silent and turned towards the sea. She remembered a stroll with her grandfather, three or four years ago, right here on this beach. They had also talked about this question, why people can't just be nice to each other.

'My granddad told me once that it's easy to love good people. The difficult part is to also love those who are bad.'

Miss God smiled and glanced at Olivia out of the corner of her eye.

'A wise man, your granddad.' She looked straight ahead again. 'However, I don't expect everyone to love each other. If you don't like someone, that's fine. But you should at least respect the other person.'

Olivia knew quite a few people she didn't like. Some of her teachers were among them, most boys from the other class and especially her cousin, who was a few years older and always treated her like a stupid baby. She was glad she didn't have to love these people. Then she thought about the woman's last remark again and suddenly had an idea.

'Maybe that's what the second commandment is all about: that all people respect each other.'

Miss God looked at her in surprise.

'That you're not mean to others and that you don't insult anyone,' Olivia continued, 'even if the other person gets on your nerves. And that you treat others the way you want to be treated yourself.'

'Brilliant!' the old woman said enthusiastically. 'What would I do without you?'

Olivia blushed. She liked receiving praise yet at the same time it often made her feel slightly uncomfortable.

'People don't have to love everyone, but they must respect each other,' Miss God summarized. 'They have to acknowledge that every person has the exact same rights, regardless of skin colour, race, gender, wealth or belief. That it's allowed and even desirable to be different.' A strong gust of wind swept across the veranda. 'And above all, people should always keep in mind that every single person is an equal in this life.'

They nodded in unison.

'And how shall we phrase the commandment?' Olivia asked.

'What about, "Respect others"?'

'Yes, that's good.'

While Miss God wrote down the two words, Olivia thought about the possible effects of this commandment.

'If everybody sticks to it, soon there will be no more wars,' she said confidently and leaned back satisfied. 'It's as simple as that.'

3
Time

hey had been sitting on the shady veranda for about half an hour already, surrounded by white sand and blue skies. Albert had fallen asleep and was softly snoring on the round carpet while Olivia sat in the comfy rocking chair, pushing the conversation ahead.

'Let's continue!'

This time it was Miss God herself who recited the next commandment.

'"Remember the Sabbath day, to keep it holy".'

She looked at her visitor expectantly.

'You're not supposed to work on Sundays and ideally you should go to church and pray,' Olivia said. There was a brief silence. Then she added: 'My grandmother actually does that, but apart from her I don't know anyone else who goes to church regularly.'

'And why do you think that is?'

Olivia thought for a moment.

'Because it's just boring.'

She had only enjoyed church once. It had been in the middle of summer, a late-morning Sunday service. She had gone with her grandmother as a favour. On that day, it was unusually hot in the church so the front door had been left open to create some ventilation. Just as the priest started his sermon, a dove flew in and got trapped inside the church. It flapped around, desperately trying to find the exit, and naturally distracted everyone from the sermon. The priest gave the bird an angry look, and shortly after that it sailed towards him, only changing course a few centimetres from his face. Whether the dove had seen his angry look was a question best reserved for a philosophical conversation, but the fact is that the little attack had forced the priest to take a quick step backwards. When the dove finally found the way out, everyone turned back to the priest and gave a start when they saw him: due to his jerky movements, his toupee had slid out of place and was now hanging above his left ear, his bald head shining on full display. Olivia didn't mind bald heads, but the image of the dangling toupee simply looked ridiculous. The children began to giggle, while the adults made discreet gestures trying to make the priest aware of the mishap. The whole spectacle lasted several minutes, and they were the best minutes Olivia had ever spent in church.

'Usually you just sit there, on an uncomfortable bench in a cold room, waiting for it to be over. The priest reads from the Bible, no one laughs, and most people don't seem very happy either. So why should you go there?'

The old woman shrugged her shoulders.

'Indeed. It's no surprise the churches are increasingly empty,' she agreed with the young girl.

'I already have to spend so many hours at school, I have to do homework and study for exams, so in my spare time I'd rather do things that I really enjoy. Like playing with friends, or watching TV, or walking with Albert.'

Miss God gave her a compassionate look.

'And my friends feel the same. Even the nerds don't like going to church, they just pretend that they do.'

'And what about your grandmother?'

Olivia stared straight ahead. Her parents weren't religious at all and even blasphemed the pope and all believers, but her grandmother always looked forward to the church ceremonies on Sundays. And she would never say anything bad about the pope or God.

'Maybe it's different for older people. After all they don't have that many friends anymore and so they go to church so that they're not alone all the time.'

'Yes, there might be some truth to this,' the old woman replied.

For a little while they were silent. Only the gentle roaring of the rolling waves was to be heard.

Olivia drank some more of her hot chocolate, then asked, 'Why is it that all priests are men? Why aren't there any women?'

Again, Miss God shrugged her shoulders.

'Probably for the same reason that nobody believes in a female God. Men are in charge, it's always been like that and they'd prefer it if it stayed that way.' She paused for a moment. 'However, I doubt that the church services would be more fun if women stood behind the pulpit.' Slowly she ran her fingers through her curls. 'They should really come up with something new. It doesn't have to be funny but at least something which isn't boring and depressing.'

Olivia nodded.

'It's a real pity,' the old woman added, 'because a church is a beautiful and special place.'

'I'm not sure,' Olivia replied sceptically. 'In the churches I know, there are huge crosses with Jesus hanging everywhere, with big nails in his hands and feet. I don't think it's very beautiful, it's rather sad.'

Miss God remained quiet, seeming to reminisce about the past.

'Once again you're right,' she finally said. 'It's such a shame because Jesus was actually a really nice guy who laughed most of the time. He would probably turn around in his grave if he knew he's still nailed to the cross, dangling in agony in so many places.'

Olivia chuckled. The old woman spoke as if she had really known Jesus. But actually, it didn't matter if it was true or just a made-up story. A laughing Jesus would definitely be much more appealing to her. And fewer crosses too.

'Why don't we simply leave out the third commandment?' she suggested. 'Many people have to work on Sundays anyway and most others feel like me: they don't want to spend their time sitting on a hard bench being bored.'

'I know what you mean,' Miss God said sympathetically. 'And yet the Sabbath commandment speaks of something very important. Especially in the modern world, where everything happens so quickly, and everyone is rushing from one place to the next, it can really help people.'

'How?'

'By taking some time out – to be with me!'

Olivia rolled her eyes.

'You mean we should spend time in prayer.'

'Exactly. That you ...' the old woman began but was interrupted at once.

'But most people don't want to pray! They don't want to go to church and they don't believe in God either. We even voted on that in school: more than half of the class said they are non-believers.'

'Is that so?'

Olivia nodded.

'And you? What did you say?'

Olivia hesitated.

'I said that I don't know.'

She looked at the ground, feeling embarrassed. It was only a game but even in the game she didn't want to disappoint the old woman. However, she showed no sign of disappointment whatsoever.

'A very good answer,' Miss God praised. 'Especially because it's an honest answer. For how could you have been sure I exist?'

Olivia looked up and saw the old woman winking at her.

'Knowing something means to be sure. For example, right now you know that I exist and even how I look. After all, I'm sitting in front of you.'

They grinned at each other.

'Believing means something different. It's more like ... like a wish! You wish that God exists. That someone has answers to all your questions and that you'll be in good company after you die. But you can't be sure. You assume that it's like that, you hope and strongly believe but you can't know it with complete certainty.'

Miss God put her pen aside.

'And since most people don't exactly know who I am, everyone can believe whatever they want. Provided of course they don't bother anyone with their beliefs and that they don't harm anyone.'

'Especially no wars!' Olivia added.

'No wars!' repeated the old woman. 'What you believe is no one else's business. It's your own, direct connection with ...'

'You.'

Miss God smiled.

'You're getting better and better! And if you want to connect with me, meaning with God, you have to pray.'

'But ...'

'Wait! I know that you don't want to go to church. You don't have to.'

Olivia breathed a sigh of relief.

'Praying is done by connecting with yourself.'

'What do you mean?'

'Remember when we talked about the first commandment? I said that all humans are a part of me. I'm connected with everybody, always! So, if you want to talk to God, you simply have to listen to what's deep inside of yourself.'

'That's all?'

'Yes. And the only thing you need to do this is some quietness.'

'So, in theory, I can pray almost anywhere, right?'

'Indeed. You can go to church or to a temple, but you can just as well pray at home in your room. You can also call it meditating. It's about calming down and listening to what your inner voice wants to tell you.'

Olivia thought this over for a moment.

'When I go for a walk with Albert, I calm down too.'

'Great! Then take him out as often as you can. Going for a walk, being in nature, admiring a sunset or staring into a fire for a while – there are many ways to connect with God.'

'But watching television is probably not one of them, is it?'

The old woman began to laugh.

'No, definitely not! And all your phones aren't either. Not that long ago, people experienced regular moments of inner peace when they were waiting for the bus or lying in bed at night. Now they're staring at some screen all the time. It's impossible to connect with yourself this way.'

'So that's why you say we should take some time out.'

'Yes, to spend time with yourself. To get to know yourself better and to be close to your own soul.'

There was stillness for a few moments.

'And what do you want to call the commandment?'

'Perhaps "Take some time for yourself"? Or even better, "Give time to yourself". Giving sounds nicer than taking.'

Olivia thought about it and rubbed her nose.

'Not bad, but it doesn't sound right yet.'

'No?'

'No.'

She rubbed her magic nose once more.

'What about "Make time for yourself"?'

Miss God's eyes began to shine.

'"Make time for yourself". Wonderful! Because, really, it's all about creating. Not giving, not taking – making! And the best thing is, when you make such a precious gift to yourself, you're automatically making the same gift to me.'

She picked up her pen and wrote down the third commandment. Olivia watched, feeling proud of herself – sometimes her ideas weren't that bad.

Then suddenly another question came to her mind.

'What exactly is a soul?'

The old woman took her eyes from the paper and inhaled deeply.

'It's the divine in you. That which makes you alive and connects you to everything.'

'When I go for a walk with Albert, I calm down too.'

'Great! Then take him out as often as you can. Going for a walk, being in nature, admiring a sunset or staring into a fire for a while – there are many ways to connect with God.'

4
Home

By now, Olivia was glad that she had accepted the invitation from Miss God. She liked the old woman, what she said and how she treated her. When Olivia spoke to other adults, she usually felt trapped in the role of the ignorant child, but this time it was an encounter with an equal. She felt taken seriously. On top of that, the sun was shining, the hot chocolate tasted delicious and the rocking chair was becoming more and more comfortable. Enough reasons to stay for a while longer.

'Ready for the next commandment?'

Olivia nodded.

'Great,' Miss God said, 'so here's number four: "Honour thy father and thy mother".'

The girl's face went dark.

'Something wrong?'

'You don't know my parents. If you did, you wouldn't like this commandment either.'

'Is it that bad?'

'Much worse than bad! They bicker and complain all the time and often they're mean to me. They punish me with house arrest and don't let me watch TV.'

'But there are probably reasons for that, aren't there?'

Olivia shrugged her shoulders.

'Maybe sometimes. But when they're annoying and exhausting, I'm not allowed to punish them. That's totally unfair.'

'Yes, you're right.'

'And they don't even do the things they expect of me themselves. For example, my Mum tells me to tidy up my room, but she should sort out her own chaos. Or my Dad – he always says I should read more and watch less TV, but he spends hours in front of the telly every night. I can't remember the last time I've seen him with a book in his hand.' Olivia began to talk herself into a rage. 'They say I shouldn't speak badly about others, but they're always gossiping; I'm always supposed to be nice and polite while they are constantly moody and unfriendly; I shouldn't fight with my cousin while they argue all day long.'

'I'm sorry about that,' Miss God sympathized. 'Unfortunately, many people act in such contradictory ways. Instead of looking at their own faults they prefer to point their finger at others.'

Olivia was still upset.

'They think that they know everything better, but they make lots of mistakes too. And when they insult me, and I defend myself, they say I'm rude and naughty.' For a moment she paused and wondered whether she should tell the old woman about what had happened the previous week. But then her doubts disappeared as quickly as they had arrived. After all it was an open and honest conversation and, even though the woman had been a stranger up until an hour or so ago, she decided to confide in her. 'The other day, during another fight, my Mum accused my Dad of not even taking the time to help me with my homework. We were just having dinner and so I was sitting next to them. I said that wasn't true because my Dad often helps me with maths. My Mum gave me an evil look and hissed at me to shut up. So, I told her to shut up herself.'

'Oh dear.' Miss God already sensed Olivia's reaction hadn't really contributed to the de-escalation of the situation. 'And then?'

'I think she would have loved to hit me. But she's only dared to do that once and afterwards I didn't speak to her for a whole week. Since then she doesn't lash out at me anymore.'

'That's something at least,' the old woman added soberly. 'Although it should be common sense not to hit children. In fact, no one should be hit.'

'Instead she yelled at me and called me an uneducated brat. She sent me to my room and forbid me to go to the cinema with my friends the next day.'

'And what did you do?'

'What could I do? Nothing. It's just so unfair!' Olivia shook her head in frustration. 'And anyway, how can she call me uneducated when she educated me herself?'

Miss God smiled a little.

'No, that's not very clever.'

Both grabbed their cups and took a long sip of their drinks. Albert continued to sleep peacefully on the round carpet.

'When I'm older I definitely don't want to become like them.'

'I understand that,' the old woman said. 'However, it's a real pity that it's like that. Because your parents could also be bright examples to you, people who inspire you and show you what is necessary to be happy. But if they aren't happy themselves that's not going to be possible.'

Olivia reflected on this for a moment. It was a nice thought, having wise role models as parents instead of grown infants.

'Maybe we should change this commandment,' she said. 'Not "Honour your father and your mother", but "Honour your children". Because it's the parents who wanted to have children and not the other way round.'

Miss God laughed out loud.

'I totally agree with you! You should be grateful to them for bringing you into the world, but you can only honour them if they act accordingly.'

They silently watched a lone seagull sail towards the ocean.

'And what about those who no longer have parents?' Olivia asked after a while. 'For them the commandment is useless anyway.'

The old woman watched the seagull for a few seconds, then she turned to her visitor and looked deep into her eyes.

'I really like that you always think of others as well. Perhaps that's something good you've learned from your parents.'

'No, definitely not from them,' Olivia said right away. 'If anyone, then from my grandmother.'

'I'd love to meet her one day, your grandmother.'

They smiled at each other. What would the world be like without the love of grandparents?

For a few moments the veranda fell silent again while Miss God ran her hands absent-mindedly through her curly hair.

'In truth, for me the fourth commandment has more to do with the roots of all humans.'

'What do you mean by the roots?'

'Where you come from,' said the old woman. 'Actually, it's not about parents and children but about our home. This planet, the Earth. Nature. Because you can live without parents but not without nature.'

This made Olivia think of her biology teacher. When he wasn't teaching them about cells and organs, he often spoke about numerous environmental problems that were getting more and more out of hand. Whenever she told her Mum about it, she'd usually say her teacher was a pessimist and that he was spreading unnecessary fear. But Olivia didn't think her teacher spread fear. He was a happy person who talked about the wonders of life with great passion. He was simply worried about the state of the world. In class, he showed them videos of cut down forests and dying bee colonies – not to scare them, but to draw their attention to problems. He always told them that a problem can only be solved once it's been accepted and understood.

'We're destroying nature, aren't we?'

Miss God nodded sadly.

'Unrenewable resources are burnt, land and air poisoned, and the oceans polluted. If you consider that the Earth is your home, it's as if you're stuffing your room with rubbish. At some point you will suffocate in it because another room, to which you could escape, doesn't exist.'

'And why do we allow that? Why don't we just clean everything up?'

The old woman sighed.

'Another one of those questions I unfortunately have no answer for. Believe me, I find it utterly frustrating myself. I gave the humans the chance to create paradise on Earth, and what do they do? They dream up paradise in heaven and turn Earth into hell.'

Depressed looks on both sides.

'Unrenewable resources are burnt, land and air poisoned, and the oceans polluted. If you consider that the Earth is your home, it's as if you're stuffing your room with rubbish. At some point you will suffocate in it because another room, to which you could escape, doesn't exist.'

'Our teacher told us that, if we continue like this, in fifty years there won't be any more fish left in the oceans. So, when I'm a grandmother, my grandchildren will only know about life in the sea from stories and films.'

'It's terrible, isn't it?' Miss God said, shaking her head.

'And on top of that, there are all the wars,' Olivia added.

'Yes, wars and many other things that bring nothing but destruction and misery. Many years ago, I withdrew completely for a while because I couldn't bear to watch all the human drama any more. Let them finish each other, I thought. But today it's different, because today humans are able to not only extinguish themselves but all other life forms as well.' She paused. 'I don't know if I will succeed but I want to at least try to prevent total annihilation.'

'That's why you're rewriting the commandments.'

'Exactly. And I also talk to people more these days, the way I'm talking to you right now.'

Olivia winced. She had forgotten it was only a game and that she was merely talking to a nice old woman. Or maybe not? What if the game wasn't a game? She almost felt ashamed for having this thought, for considering such a possibility at all. But as crazy as it sounded, why shouldn't this possibility exist?

She decided to ask the woman a question that only God would be able to answer.

'Was Jesus really your son?'

She was met with a puzzled look.

'Why do you want to know that?'

'I just do.'

Miss God leaned back and seemed to carefully think about how she should answer.

'Jesus was a wonderful man with a big heart. I liked him a lot and he shared many wise words. For example, he always said that the realm of God is right amongst us. With that he expressed exactly what we've just talked about: that paradise is directly at our feet and not somewhere far beyond the stars.'

'But was he your son or not?' Olivia persisted.

Another long pause. Then the old woman smiled.

'Yes, he was my son. Just like you are my daughter.'

The girl rolled her eyes again.

'But I'm not your daughter.'

'How come you're so sure about that?'

'Because ...'

Now it was Olivia who hesitated. Actually, being the daughter of God didn't seem so bad, she thought, then at least she'd get rid of her annoying parents. But she probably wouldn't be that lucky. No, unfortunately it was just a game.

'At the end of the day it's not so important who your parents are and whether they are still alive or not,' the old woman continued after a while. 'Our home is the Earth. For me, for you and for everyone else too.'

'Then we shouldn't honour the parents but the Earth.'

'Yes! We should care for her, respect her, appreciate and love her. And most of all we should always remember that it's her who makes life possible for us.'

A fresh breeze touched their cheeks and blew some sand on to the wooden floor. Olivia stared into nothingness for a moment.

'Is that the reason why we say Mother Nature?' she asked. 'Because nature is our true mother?'

Miss God answered with another smile. Then she silently took the pen into her hand and wrote a couple of words under the last commandment. When she was done, she turned the notepad to her guest.

'Okay?'

'"Honour nature",' Olivia read aloud. She nodded and visualized planet Earth floating in space. What a beautiful home it was, she thought. And what a shame that so many people treated this home like a rubbish bin.

'Best to underline this commandment!' she added.

5
Peace

ome of the sand that had blown on to the veranda had reached Albert's nose and woken him up. He sneezed once, got up and shook himself. Then, still half asleep, he dragged himself to the water bowl and calmly took a few sips. When he had quenched his thirst, he turned to Olivia expectantly. Luckily, she had already forgotten that he had ignored her earlier and so he received the petting he had hoped for. Joyfully, he began to wag his tail. As Olivia gently scratched him behind the ears, his wagging got wilder and wilder. And then it happened: his tail hit the yellow cup that had been standing on the floor and knocked it over with a loud bang. The rest of the hot chocolate spilled and spread out underneath the rocking chair.

'Albert!' Olivia shouted and jumped up. 'Just look at what you've done!'

Angrily she pretended to kick him, causing the little terrier to run away and hide on the other side of the veranda. Olivia pushed back the chair and picked up the cup.

'I'm really sorry,' she said to the old woman.

'No problem. I've lived with dogs before. For some reason they never properly learned to control their backsides.'

She got up and collected both Olivia's cup and her own.

'Do you want another hot chocolate?'

'I'd love one.'

Miss God went into the hut, placed a pot of milk on the stove and returned with a wet cloth. Olivia wanted to take it from her but the old woman was quicker and had already bent down to start mopping up the mess.

'I may not be the youngest but I can still just about handle this myself,' she said with a wink of her eye.

Shortly afterwards the floor was clean again and Miss God went back into the kitchen. Olivia moved the rocking chair into its place and let herself fall into it. Her mother had never reacted this calmly when Albert knocked over glasses and vases at home. She'd usually scream at her and then Olivia would pass her Mum's anger on to her dog.

She looked at him as he crouched in the far corner, well aware that he had done something wrong.

'I know,' she finally said, 'you didn't do it on purpose.'

She made a sign with her hand and Albert came running immediately. His tail was now so out of control he was hitting his own hips.

'But sit down, otherwise you'll knock something else over.'

Albert obeyed and lay down next to her chair.

'Would you like some cream on top?' Miss God shouted from the kitchen.

'Yes, please!'

She could hear the sound of a blender, and a little while later, the old woman came back with two cups, both topped with a mountain of white cream. She handed one to her visitor and placed the other on the bench. Then she disappeared inside again and returned with a plate full of biscuits.

'Philosophizing is hard work,' she said. 'Here, help yourself!'

Olivia grabbed one of the biscuits, dipped it into the cream and took a big bite. Her eyes lit up.

'Yummy,' she mumbled with a full mouth.

'Freshly baked this morning. Take some more if you want.'

Olivia didn't have to be told twice; she grabbed another handful of the golden treasures and put them on her lap. The old woman placed the plate on the bench, sat down and dipped a biscuit into her drink too.

'I usually prefer to drink herbal teas, but sometimes there's nothing better than a hot chocolate with cream and cookies.'

They relaxed and enjoyed their little treats for a while.

'Shall we continue?'

'Okay.'

'So next we have the killing ban,' Miss God said, immediately adding: 'Of all commandments I find this one to be the most unnecessary.'

'Why?' Olivia replied, with a look of astonishment. '"Do not murder" – that's super important!'

'Yes, it's important, but really it shouldn't be necessary to have to say it. Sure, there are problems and disagreements and every now and then perhaps even a bigger fight, but how is it possible that people end up killing each other? I don't understand that.'

Olivia shrugged her shoulders. She didn't really understand it either. When her cousin was mean to her, she often felt the desire to pay it back, to hurt her as much as possible, but it only happened in her imagination. And even though she had wished the stupid cow would disappear into the afterworld on many occasions, it would have never occurred to her to actually kill her cousin.

'To end the life of someone else, violently and on purpose, is the biggest crime a human being can commit. There is no justification for this and no excuse either.' Miss God shook her head angrily. 'It's really unbelievable that these things are still happening on a daily basis. Entire countries happily kill and yet they have the audacity to call themselves civilized.'

Olivia stuffed another biscuit into her mouth. She hadn't really heard the last sentences because her thoughts had got stuck at what it means to reach the end of your life.

'What happens when we die?' she wanted to know.

Miss God also reached for another biscuit and fell silent for a few moments.

'What would you like? I mean, if you could choose what happens to you after death.'

'No idea,' Olivia said. 'What can I choose from?'

'Let's see ...' The old woman stirred her hot chocolate. 'There's the idea of heaven and hell, which means that if all goes well, you'd end up happily sitting on a cloud with all your dead friends.'

Olivia thought of her uncle and her grandfather. It would be nice to see them again.

'You could also go to paradise where there are rivers of milk and honey and you'd have lots of servants. Or you could be reborn, as another person or a cat or a mosquito.'

'As a mosquito? No, I don't want that.'

'Alright, I can also offer the great big nothingness. A huge black hole, empty and dark.'

'I can't imagine that, complete nothingness. There must be something that still exists.' She paused and thought about the first two options again. 'I'm sure heaven wouldn't be bad but I don't think we'd be living on clouds. And rivers of milk and honey? No.'

Both drank their hot chocolate. Olivia continued to mull over her different options.

'Do all people go to the same place when they're dead?'

She received a surprised look.

'Do you really think there are different areas for Catholics, Jews and Muslims in the afterworld? One for good souls and one for bad ones? Women to the left, men to the right?'

Olivia shook her head. No, that didn't make much sense.

'Can't you just tell me what happens?' she asked, growing a little impatient. 'I won't guess it anyway.'

The old woman hesitated.

'Why do you want to know so badly? Are you afraid of death?'

'No, not really. But I'd like to know where we go to.'

'And what would it change?'

'I don't know. I'm just curious.'

'But imagine that I tell you after death comes the great nothingness. Or something else you don't like. Then perhaps you would get scared.'

Olivia moved her mouth from side to side thinking about it.

'And what if there were something nice awaiting me after death? Then I could look forward to it.'

Miss God smiled.

'Just let yourself be surprised. Or don't you like surprises?'

'Yes, but ...'

She didn't know what to say. Why was the woman so secretive about it? It was probably just more evidence that she wasn't God at all, otherwise she would have given her a clear answer by now.

'In the first commandment we said that I am life.'

'You?'

'Yes, me. God.'

The old woman spoke with total conviction, not the slightest hint of doubt noticeable in her voice. She's a really good actress, Olivia thought, you have to give her that.

'God is life,' the old woman continued, 'and life happens here and now. However, when you think about death, about what happens when you die, then your thoughts are in the future. And when you're in the future, you miss the present. You're somewhere, but not right here in this moment.'

Olivia wasn't completely satisfied yet.

'Knowing what happens after death would only distract you from life,' Miss God explained.

'I understand this but ... Can't you give me a little hint anyway?'

The old woman grinned at her.

'You're pretty persistent. But it wouldn't be fair to all the other people because I've never told anyone. You would know something that no one else knows.'

'That's exactly what I want!'

The old woman laughed.

'Look, I won't tell you exactly what happens, but I will give you another alternative to heaven, rebirth and the big black hole. Then you can pick your favourite and believe whatever you want. Okay?'

Olivia nodded. Better than nothing.

'Imagine that every being is a drop of water. There are big ones and small ones, some are murky and others are crystal clear. Every drop feels like an independent drop, separated from all the other drops, but all drops ...'

'... are water.'

'Yes, and where does all water end up sooner or later?'

They both looked across the dune towards the horizon.

'In the sea.'

'That's right. The drops won't be drops any more but they will continue to be water.'

Olivia liked the idea of transmuting into the sea.

'But eventually the sea water will turn into rain and then there will be new drops again,' she thought out loud. 'So really it's very similar to the idea of rebirth.'

'A bit, yes,' Miss God said and let out a little sigh. 'The problem is that you humans think everything must have a beginning and an end. But with life itself it's not the case. Death isn't the end, it's merely a part of the whole. Single drops disappear but life always continues.'

'So that's what happens?'

'Nice try,' the old woman laughed. 'I told you that I would only give you another option. You have to decide what you want to believe for yourself.'

'And how am I supposed to decide?'

'Just believe whatever feels best to you.'

'Alright then,' Olivia gave in, but the disappointment of not having received a definite answer was written all over her face.

Miss God gave her a warm smile.

'I can tell you this much: the world that awaits you after death is not an unknown world. It will feel a bit like coming home.'

Now Olivia smiled too. Dying is like coming home, more than that she didn't need to know. She got up and took some more biscuits from the plate.

'They're really delicious!'

A few crumbs landed on the floor and immediately attracted the little terrier's attention. He stretched to reach the crumbs and lapped them up with great relish. Olivia watched him and suddenly felt a heaviness in her heart.

'Imagine that every being is a drop of water. There are big ones and small ones, some are murky and others are crystal clear. Every drop feels like an independent drop, separated from all the other drops, but all drops ...'

'... are water.'

'What about animals? Why aren't they included in the murder commandment?'

'I didn't say that animals aren't included.'

'But then it should be forbidden to eat them.'

Miss God nodded silently.

'A wise man once said that people will only find true peace when there are no more slaughterhouses. I completely agree with him.'

Olivia thought of two of her classmates who were vegetarians and felt a sting of envy. She had asked her parents to buy less fish and meat many times but, as so often, it was hopeless with them. If she didn't want to go hungry, she had no choice but to continue eating chickens, cows, pigs and salmon. At least for now. She already longed for the day when she would be able to decide for herself whether to eat meat or not.

'You know,' the old woman continued in a sad voice, 'unfortunately, all the slaughter and murder is only the tip of a huge iceberg, an iceberg called violence. Because people aren't only violent when they kill but also with lots of other things they do. They oppress, rob, insult and abuse. They exploit fellow human beings, torture animals and rape nature. They lash out with hands and words and don't stop short at anything. Not only do they harm strangers but also their neighbours and even their own children.'

Olivia lowered her eyes to the ground.

'So much violence ... I wonder where it comes from?'

Silence.

'Do you really want to know?'

'Of course.'

Miss God calmly put down her cup.

'Alright. The origin of violence lies right here.'

She pointed her finger at her chest.

'In your heart?'

'Yes. And in yours too.'

'In mine?' Olivia was alarmed. 'But why?'

'Because everyone gets hurt in life.'

'I don't think I was ever hurt by anyone.'

'Are you sure? No one has ever insulted you? Your parents have never treated you unfairly and you've never felt great sadness seeing images of war?'

Miss God was met with silence.

'Or when your grandfather died, and you felt disappointed by life, didn't that hurt?'

Olivia turned to the old woman, eyes wide open. How did she know about that?

'All these painful feelings leave wounds in your heart. And if you don't heal these wounds, they get infected and cause more pain.' The old woman paused for a moment. 'That's why people are violent, because their pain screams for revenge and keeps them from being peaceful.'

'And how can I heal the wounds in my heart?'

Miss God smiled at her affectionately.

'By forgiving.'

'Sometimes that's quite difficult though.'

'No, it's actually not that difficult at all. And even if it were, it's the only way to end violence amongst humans. Because as long as you can't forgive, you won't find inner peace, and without inner peace there can be no peaceful world either.'

What the old woman said made sense, but Olivia didn't really know how to tackle this mammoth task.

'But how do I forgive?'

'It's best to start with yourself. Forgive yourself for the mistakes you've made, the evil things you've said and thought and all the bad feelings you've guarded. And most importantly, don't be afraid because nobody does everything right. Everyone still has a lot to learn, even me.'

She winked at the girl.

'But I still haven't quite understood how to do this,' Olivia said, feeling frustrated and helpless. 'How can I learn to forgive?'

Miss God took a few deep breaths and briefly closed her eyes. Then she looked at Olivia again.

'Start by letting go of the past.'

'Just like that?'

'Yes, just like that. Whatever happened yesterday doesn't exist anymore. Why would you want to hold on to it?'

Olivia shrugged her shoulders. She wasn't sure if it really was as simple as the woman made it out to be, but of course she wasn't completely wrong. Somehow all these wounds had to heal, otherwise there would never be peace.

She shoved another biscuit into her mouth and devoured it in no time.

'"Forgive". I think that's what the fifth commandment should say.'

Miss God looked at her in astonishment, and then took time to contemplate Olivia's suggestion.

'It's actually perfect,' she finally said. 'A call for forgiveness is much better than a killing ban, because it addresses the real cause of the problem rather than only a symptom.'

Thrilled, Miss God reached for the pen. Then suddenly a doubt seemed to cross her mind.

'But don't you think one word is too little?'

Olivia shook her head.

'Not if it's such an important word.'

6
Friendship

he wind picked up and more clouds appeared in the sky. It was still a nice afternoon, but signs increasingly suggested it might not stay this way. Olivia zipped up her hoodie and slipped her hands into its pockets.

'Number six,' Miss God said. '"Thou shalt not commit adultery". So, basically you shouldn't end marriage.'

'This one relates to my parents again,' Olivia sighed.

'Your favourite subject, right?'

They both grinned.

'What a silly commandment! Why shouldn't you be allowed to end a marriage?'

'I agree, it shouldn't be forbidden. However, perhaps it's not always the best idea to get divorced just because you're having a few problems. Because together you can solve them too, most of the time even much better. And although your parents fight a lot, wouldn't you feel sad if they separated?'

'Sad?' Olivia began to laugh. 'I would jump with joy!'

'Okay. But why do you think they fight so much?'

Olivia was silent for a moment.

'They're simply too different. My Dad enjoys peace and quiet, my Mum loves hustle and bustle. He's tidy, she's chaotic; he's constantly cold, she's always too warm. And on top of that, there's the problem with the volume.'

'The volume?'

'Yes. My Mum has a very loud voice, even when she speaks normally. And my Dad has very sensitive hearing.' She dropped her shoulders in consternation. 'They just don't fit together at all! It's like a goldfish being married to a parrot.'

'No, that's not a good fit,' Miss God agreed with a little smile.

Olivia had given up on the hope that the relationship between her parents might improve one day, at least not as long as they were living under the same roof. Their interests and needs, their personalities, their views and their dreams were too different. Sometimes she felt the only reason why they hadn't divorced was to not disappoint their daughter and plunge her into a depression. But in reality, the opposite was the case.

'If they separated, everyone would be happier: my father, my mother and especially me. Even Albert would be glad.'

She glanced down at where her dog had been lying, but to her surprise he was neither in the spot next to the chair nor anywhere else.

'Maybe he had to stretch his legs,' Miss God said.

Olivia got up and scanned the sand dune. Nothing.

'Albert?' she shouted, but there was still no sign of him.

'He'll probably be back soon.'

For sure, Olivia thought, but she still wanted to know where he was. She crossed the veranda and walked around the hut. When she arrived at the back, she finally spotted him: he was squatting in the middle of a big field doing his business. Olivia turned around and left him to it. On the way back, she noticed a surfboard leaning against the side of the hut.

'You were right, he had to stretch his legs,' she said when she returned to the old woman. 'Whose surfboard is that?'

'Mine.'

'You surf?'

Miss God nodded euphorically.

'It's my big passion! There's nothing better than riding a wave under the setting sun.'

'But ...'

'What? Am I too old for that?'

'No, of course not,' Olivia back-pedalled. 'You just don't look like a typical surfer.'

'Oh, so what does a typical surfer look like?' Miss God asked, almost sounding a bit offended.

'Just different. Not like an old woman in a dress.'

Miss God shook her head.

'I'm not allowed to surf, I'm not allowed to be God. What else?'

'I don't mean it in a bad way,' Olivia said apologetically.

'I know that. But it's still a problem.'

'Why is it a problem?'

The old woman reached for her cup and drank a few sips.

'There are set ideas in your minds which prevent you people from evolving and enjoying life to the fullest.'

Olivia looked at her in confusion.

'Just because you have never seen an old woman on a surfboard, doesn't mean that old women can't surf with great joy. And that's exactly why so few old women surf – because they think it's not possible.' She paused. 'If I were an old man, you probably wouldn't have been so astonished, right?'

'Probably not,' Olivia admitted.

The old woman shook her head again, then smiled in a motherly way.

'I guess it's what they teach you. For thousands of years women have been regarded as weaker and dumber, always second behind men. And even in the Bible, in the holy scripture of God, this inequality is confirmed. Eve was made to help Adam, that's what Moses apparently said.'

'Didn't he?'

'No, he didn't. He said that Eve and Adam were made to help – each other! But like so often, someone changed and totally distorted my original message. It really drives me up the wall!'

Miss God didn't sound very pleased.

'Unfortunately, that's only one example of many. How dare these people spread such nonsense? Believe me, if I were really able to decide on people's lives and if hell really existed, these swindlers would roast there for all eternity.'

She received a slightly shocked glance from Olivia.

'Okay, perhaps not for all eternity. But these wrong interpretations are causing a lot of harm.'

'I don't think it's as bad as it used to be though. Nowadays women and men are treated almost equally.'

'And why only almost?'

Olivia didn't know. It was a good question.

'Of course lots of things have improved, but things are far from being as they should be. And occasionally you still find extremely contemptuous opinions that have survived to this day. Just the other week I read that men and women are worth the same but don't have equal rights, in a little booklet from a Christian organization. It said that the man not only has the right but the duty to rule over his wife. If he doesn't rule over her, he is committing a sin before God.'

The old woman looked into Olivia's eyes, speechless for a moment.

'What a disgrace to be linking me to such a statement!'

Indeed, that wasn't very nice. Olivia could understand her anger, even though she didn't think it was all that dramatic herself. At least she'd never heard anyone mention such barbarities.

'But most people don't think like this anymore.'

'No, fortunately not. And yet there are still far too many hidden remnants of this kind of thinking. Especially in our language. For example, take the word "mankind". Man-kind. Why doesn't it say woman-kind?'

Olivia laughed out loud.

'Because it sounds stupid!'

Miss God had to laugh as well, but quickly turned serious again.

'And why does it sound stupid?'

'Because it just sounds weird.'

'Yes, but why?'

'I don't know. Why?'

The old woman took a deep breath.

'Because you're not used to it. That's all.' She contemplated for a moment. 'What are those photos called again, the ones you take of yourselves with your mobile phones?'

'Selfies.'

'Just because you have never seen an old woman on a surfboard, doesn't mean that old women can't surf with great joy. And that's exactly why so few old women surf – because they think it's not possible.'

'That's right, selfies. Ten years ago, that word didn't even exist. If you had used it back then, everyone would have laughed at you. However, today it sounds normal, doesn't it?'

Olivia nodded.

'But to say womankind instead of mankind ... seriously?'

She couldn't really warm to this idea.

'Well, it's not that we have to change every word now. But if you understand how language has been influenced by men, you'll also become more aware of how our thinking has been manipulated. Often these are only little details, but many little details combined have a huge impact.'

'Such as?'

'Just look at society: most experts, heroes and presidents are men. Do you think this is a coincidence? Do you think that women don't want to be heroines and that they are not capable of governing countries?'

Olivia shook her head.

'You're right, it's not as bad as it used to be,' the old woman continued. 'But there's still a long way to go before the amazement stops every time a woman knows more than a man, and business-leading women are no longer doubted. And vice versa it's similar, because most men are still belittled when they stay home to take care of the children while the woman goes to work.'

Olivia wouldn't actually mind if both her parents went to work. That way at least the afternoons at home would be peaceful.

Albert returned from his excursion and lay down on the colourful, round carpet again. The other two drank some more hot chocolate.

'You know,' Miss God said after a while, 'there are of course big differences between men and women, but at the end of the day they're all humans. All are worth the same and therefore all should be equally free and have the same opportunities. And that brings us straight back to marriage, because for a relationship to be healthy it's extremely important that both partners recognize they have the same rights. Without this as a basis, it doesn't work.'

'And what if they still fight all the time?'

'If the problems don't decrease, it's indeed better to go separate ways. Continuous hostility is definitely no solution.'

Olivia thought of one of her classmates, whose parents had been as bad as her own. One year ago they got divorced and since then everything was much better. They could talk to each other again without screaming every few minutes, and sometimes they even smile at each other.

'Maybe my parents would become friends if they weren't together anymore.'

'Sure, why not? I suppose when they met they were friends too. Perhaps they've simply changed over time. That's totally normal, all people change. Every person has their own experiences in life and learns different things, and through these experiences everyone changes, every single day! So, if two people have evolved differently and don't have much in common anymore, it's completely natural. The question is, how do they deal with the new situation?' The old woman paused. 'No, I'm not against divorce. But I'm against unhappy divorce!'

'Unhappy divorce?'

'Yes, when the fight continues even after the separation.'

Olivia felt slightly worried. What if her parents never stopped bickering?

'In that case the fifth commandment would be helpful,' Miss God said. 'To "forgive"! To let go of the past, close the chapter and move on.'

'It doesn't sound that difficult,' Olivia said.

'It isn't. But for some reason humans always seem to need an enemy. Either it's the partner or the ex-partner, the opposing football team, the political rival or the rogue state on the other side of the world. And of course, not to forget all the religions that hate each other. Who is supposed to make sense of that?'

Olivia shrugged her shoulders.

'If Jesus, Buddha and Mohammed had lived at the same time and had met, I'm very sure that they would have become good friends. But unfortunately, hardly anyone considers such a possibility. It's really sad.'

Olivia could only agree. However, she had noticed something else that she didn't agree with.

'Jesus, Buddha, Mohammed – why are they all men? Why didn't you talk to women too?'

'Well spotted!' Miss God said, praising her. 'Of course I've also spoken to women. The problem is that no one tells their stories and so they remain unknown. I hope it will be different with you.'

She winked at her. Olivia wanted to roll her eyes again but decided to keep playing.

'I hope so too.'

She received a satisfied smile. Game or not, both felt that it was long overdue to fill the history books with more women.

'So, what are we going to do with this commandment?' Miss God asked after a little while.

'No idea.'

'I think I wrote something down a few days ago.' She flicked through her notepad. 'Ah, here: "Keep your word",' she read. 'What do you think?'

'Hmm, I don't know.'

'It only works if nothing is promised that can't be kept. If two people get married and vow to each other to always stay together, it might be a nice romantic moment, but in reality it's just wishful thinking. It would be better to promise to always respect each other. Regardless of whether the marriage lasts or not.'

Olivia seemed a little less sceptical now.

'And it's not just important in marriage, but also in friendship, in business and in any other relationship between people. If you give someone your word, you have to keep it. Otherwise words will become worthless one day.'

A ray of sunlight peaked through under the roof of the veranda.

'"Keep your word",' Olivia thought aloud. The old woman was certainly right. It's important to be able to rely on the promises of others. But whether it was important enough to be one of the Ten Commandments, of that Olivia wasn't so sure. However, she couldn't find any good reasons against it and she couldn't think of anything better either.

'Fine. Let's go with that.'

What had Miss God said earlier? Let go and move on.

7
Compassion

livia wondered how long she had been sitting with the old woman. On one hand she felt that their conversation had only just begun, but on the other hand it already seemed to be lasting an eternity.

'Do you know what time it is?' she asked.

Miss God leaned forward and looked at the sky. The sun had started its slow descent towards the sea.

'Perhaps four? Or five?'

Olivia wasn't surprised at all to see the old woman using the sky as her clock. She herself owned a mobile phone, like almost all children her age, but when she had escaped her parents' fighting, she had left it on her bed.

'I think I have to go back soon.'

'No problem,' the old woman replied. 'Let's see if we can do one or two more commandments and then we'll stop.'

Olivia nodded in agreement. In a way, she wouldn't have minded staying in the comfortable rocking chair the rest of the day, but her parents wanted to head home in the evening and if she didn't show up on time, she'd surely get into trouble. And she didn't want her parents to worry about her either.

'Alright,' Miss God said. 'Number seven. Do you remember how it goes?'

'"Thou shalt not steal",' Olivia answered, wrinkling her nose.

'What's the matter?'

'It's so ... unnecessary.'

'You think so?'

'Yes. It should go without saying that we don't steal.'

Miss God let out a long sigh.

'We've been over this before. If we look at what should be obvious, many commandments are unnecessary. Especially the murder one! But whether it's stealing or killing, sadly these things happen in the world.'

'Has it always been like that?' Olivia asked.

The old woman thought for a moment.

'I'm afraid so. In the past it just wasn't as noticeable because there were fewer people around. But humans have always made each other's lives difficult, they have killed and robbed for thousands of years. It's almost as though evil is something people need.'

'But why should they need it?'

Another sigh from the old woman.

'I don't know.'

Olivia eyed her with suspicion.

'Considering you're God, there are quite a lot of things you don't know.'

'Why do you still think I should know everything?'

'Well, somebody needs to know,' Olivia countered. 'And if not God, who else?'

The old woman shifted her head from side to side as if she didn't know whether to agree or to object. Then she looked at the ground, slightly embarrassed.

'Something just went wrong,' she murmured to herself.

'What do you mean?'

'The Creation. Something went wrong with it.'

'What?'

Miss God shrugged her shoulders, helplessly.

'I thought I had done everything right. Beautiful, fertile landscapes, many unique creatures, constant evolution – a diversified, wonderful world! In addition to that I came up with lots of things to make humans enjoy this wonderful world even better. For example, the five senses, a flexible body and a vivid mind. They can think, wonder, dream, laugh and love.'

'But these are all good things,' Olivia said.

'Yes, they are.' The old woman hesitated. 'However, there are two other things I probably should have left out: fear and free will.'

Miss God stared into Olivia's waiting eyes. She took a deep breath and continued.

'Free will was actually a good idea. I was convinced that, if I gave humans complete self-determination, they would always strive to be happy together and to care for and protect this wonderful world. Unfortunately, this hasn't happened, and I think a lot of it has to do with fear. We've already seen this in the second commandment: they are scared of poverty, of the unknown and especially of the future. And because they fear so much, they hardly have any time left to love.'

They looked at each other with sadness. Then Olivia began to shake her head.

'So why did you create fear in the first place?' she asked, almost a little upset.

'I thought it might be helpful. So that people are careful when they walk along a precipice or when a hungry tiger is nearby. I never imagined that fear could spread to all other life situations. It's like a wildfire that has got totally out of control!'

'Can't you simply take the fear away again?'

The old woman smiled.

'That would be nice, wouldn't it?'

She silently regarded her visitor for a while.

'If I hadn't given them free will, perhaps I would be able to do something about it, but not like this.' Again, a short silence. 'No, humans are fully responsible for themselves! And so, to defeat evil, every single person has to start choosing love over fear.'

Miss God grabbed her cup, stirred the hot chocolate a few times and took a big sip. She seemed pleased with her explanation. Olivia wasn't as impressed.

'I understand the fear and love thing and that we have to decide for ourselves. But what if something bad happens even though you've chosen love?'

The neighbours' boy came to her mind again, like he had several times that afternoon.

'My friend from next door suddenly went blind when he was six years old. He had always been nice and friendly, yet still it happened. Why?'

The old woman shifted around the bench nervously and stared into nothingness. It was an awkward question to which even God didn't have a convincing answer.

'The Hindus explain it with rebirth and karma. They say that if you do something bad in your present life, you'll be punished for it in the next life.'

'But I'm not a Hindu. And I'm not sure I believe in rebirth either.'

Miss God sighed again and took another sip of her drink, before fixing Olivia with a compassionate look.

'I know you think it's unfair that your neighbour went blind. Believe me, I don't think it's fair either and if I could change it, I would do so right away.' She paused. 'I also understand that people lose faith in me when they experience a lot of pain that they can't explain. Like when someone goes blind, or your own child dies or when a dear friend suffers from a mysterious illness. But once again: I created the humans, but I don't decide what happens to them. I don't punish anyone, and I certainly haven't stolen your friend's eyesight.'

'So why did it happen?'

Olivia wouldn't give up.

'Perhaps he had something to learn.'

'Like what?'

The old woman shrugged her shoulders.

'I don't know exactly.'

Olivia liked the fact that God wasn't an all-knowing being and yet, she was a little disappointed. She let her mind wander and soon her thoughts led to her communion class.

'Our priest told us that people suffer because they have to pay for the sin of Eve.'

The old woman looked at her with wide eyes.

'Just because she ate an apple?'

This time it was Olivia who shrugged her shoulders.

'So why did you create fear
in the first place?' she asked,
almost a little upset.

'I thought it might be helpful.
So that people are careful when they
walk along a precipice or when
a hungry tiger is nearby.
I never imagined that fear could
spread to all other life situations.
It's like a wildfire that has
got totally out of control!'

'Some of the stories you humans come up with are really weird,' Miss God said with a shake of her head.

They each took another biscuit.

Silence.

'You know,' the old woman continued after a while, 'there isn't always an obvious answer for every question. Often it takes some time to discover a deeper meaning and to understand why something is happening. It might be that a stroke of fate appears like a bad curse at first, but then later on it turns out to be a blessing.'

Olivia studied her thoughtfully. She wasn't completely convinced yet.

'Maybe your neighbour will develop a great sense of hearing due to his blindness and will become a gifted musician,' Miss God continued. 'Or he will become an excellent psychologist because he can focus on listening better. Or perhaps he will simply help to remind others how amazing it is to be able to see.'

'And what if none of this occurs?'

Again silence.

'You're right, this can happen too. For some questions you might never find a good answer, no matter how long you look for it. I think in such cases there's nothing else you can do apart from accepting life as it is. With all the good and bad sides. It's not easy but sometimes it's the only thing you can do.'

They looked at the horizon again. No, life wasn't always easy.

'But luckily such cases are the exceptions,' the old woman finally said in an encouraging voice. 'Most of the time people can indeed transform evil into good. And that's what the Ten Commandments are all about: to humbly accept what you can't change, and to change what you don't have to accept.'

Olivia turned to her and smiled.

'Like stealing! We don't have to accept that,' Olivia said.

'Exactly! And theft doesn't only refer to physical property, like a bicycle, jewellery, money or some chewing gum. Especially nowadays, many things that you can't touch directly are stolen, like words, songs and photos. Small and big works of art many people use on a daily basis – without asking for permission or paying for it.'

Olivia bit her lip. She listened to music on her phone every day and she had never paid a single penny for it. So strictly speaking she was also a thief. And then she remembered the book she had borrowed from her best friend and hadn't given back in over a year. Was that theft too, borrowing for too long? It was one of her favourite books and she wanted to read it for a third time. The story of Momo, a young girl, and her fight against the grey gentlemen who steal hours from the people.

'You can also steal time,' she said.

'Indeed!' Miss God replied at once. 'Unfortunately, this is a daily occurrence as well. When you annoy people even though they'd like a moment of peace, or when you are late and keep someone waiting.'

Again, Olivia found she wasn't completely innocent. Punctuality was definitely not her strong suit.

'Lots of stealing also happens when people go shopping,' the old woman continued. 'Because when you choose the cheapest chocolate, you know the farmer will only get paid a pittance for his hard work. And it's the same with almost all products, be it food, clothing or phones. It's only cheap because somewhere, someone is being exploited. And exploitation is ultimately just a different form of stealing.' She took a deep breath. 'And don't get me started on kings, politicians and bankers, for they are the true masters of theft!'

Olivia let her eyes wander until they reached Albert. Her little terrier was lying on the round carpet and had fallen asleep again.

'And how can we make it better?'

'Well, the best thing would be of course to simply stop stealing,' Miss God replied. 'To pay fair prices and to not take anything from anyone without asking. Just like it says in the seventh commandment.'

'So far this hasn't really worked though,' Olivia noted soberly.

'No, it hasn't.'

They fell silent and thought about how to rephrase the commandment so that it would have a better effect. While Olivia pondered, her attention was drawn to the plate on the bench next to the old woman. A single biscuit was left and it seemed to beckon her to be eaten. Suddenly she had an idea.

'What about using the opposite of stealing?'

Miss God looked up, surprised.

'The opposite?'

Olivia got up, took two steps to the bench and picked up the last biscuit. She broke it in half and gave one part to the old woman.

'Not stealing but sharing.'

As if in slow motion, Miss God took half the biscuit and stared at the girl, speechless. Then she beamed at her.

'Not stealing but sharing – you're a genius!'

Olivia blushed.

'No, I'm not,' she said modestly.

'Yes, you are! If your ideas are better than God's, you must be a genius.' The old woman winked at her. But her admiration was sincere.

'Hearing what you think and seeing who you are, I wonder whether I should have omitted adults. After all, everything bad and evil is done by them. A world with only children would surely be a better world, don't you think?'

'But I also know lots of idiots my age,' the girl said. 'Children who are mean and selfish.'

'I guess you're right. They're probably just too small to cause any bigger damage. And we can't forget there are also adults who are predominantly peaceful and helpful. People who give more than they take, who have understood that happiness grows when it's shared.'

They ate the last biscuit and smiled at each other.

'You can share everything,' Olivia said when she had swallowed the last crumbs. 'Food and games, money and time, love and happiness. Even tears can be shared.'

'Yes, even tears.'

A breath of magic blew across the veranda and they both dreamed of a world in which people stuck together at all times and the good always prevailed over the bad.

'Jesus and I also talked about compassion and the courage to be generous,' Miss God recalled. 'Later on in his life, he often preached that sharing is one of our most powerful weapons against evil. For sharing is love in its purest form.'

Olivia stared at her in disbelief. Not because of the sharing part, but because of the story.

'Okay, be honest: Jesus, Mary and Moses, did they really exist?'

The old woman smiled.

'If you want, we can discuss that during the next commandment, which is all about lies and truth. But first, let's finish rephrasing the stealing commandment.'

'But we've already done that.'

'Have we?'

'Yes,' Olivia said. '"Share!"'

8
Truth

nce Miss God had written down the new version of the seventh commandment, she put pen and paper aside and immediately moved on to the next.

'Number eight: "Thou shalt not bear false witness against thy neighbour".'

Olivia let out a painful moan, as if she were suffering in great agony.

'Everything alright?' the old woman asked.

'No, it's horrible.'

'What is?'

'The commandment! Who talks like this? And who is supposed to understand it?'

'You don't understand it?'

'Yes, I do. But only because we talked about it at school and in communion class. Normally, I would skip over such a sentence right away.' She shook her head. 'Why so complicated? Why doesn't it simply say, "Don't lie"?'

'That's how they expressed themselves back then. I can't really tell you why no one has changed it until now.'

Olivia shook her head again. Then she suddenly remembered her question.

'So: Jesus, Mary, Moses and all the other saints – was it all a lie or did they really exist?'

'Does it matter if they existed?'

'No, but I would like to know anyway,' Olivia persisted. 'Priests always say that the Bible holds the truth. Is that so?'

'Yes, there's lots of truth in the Bible,' Miss God said. 'But whether the stories are true?'

She fell silent and looked into Olivia's expectant eyes.

'Yes or no?' the girl urged.

'Some are true, others not.'

Olivia sighed loudly. Why was it so difficult to get a straight answer out of this woman? Perhaps she had to form her question more precisely.

'Jesus, did he exist or not?'

'Yes.'

Finally, she thought.

'But not all stories that are told about Jesus really happened,' the old woman added.

'So which ones are true? The one with the resurrection? The miracles he performed? The long beard?'

'He did actually have that long beard,' Miss God laughed. 'But everything else is only of secondary importance. What matters are his words about love, friendship and mercy. His message, that's what is true.'

Olivia smiled. She liked that last bit, even though she had hoped for a different answer. She sighed again. It was probably pointless to continue trying to get historical secrets from the old woman. Either she simply couldn't tell her more because she didn't know herself, since she wasn't God, or she didn't want to tell her more. By now Olivia was so immersed in the role play that she considered the second option as realistic too. Who knows, she thought, maybe it's better if certain things remain a mystery.

She took her hot chocolate and drank the last sips of the delicious brew. Then she set down the cup next to her, let herself sink back into the rocking chair and brought her thoughts back to the eighth commandment.

'Why do people lie so much?' she asked.

'That's a good question,' Miss God replied. 'Let's start with you: why do you lie?'

'Me?'

Olivia stared at her with a mixture of indignation and innocence.

'Yes, you.'

'But I don't lie.'

'Are you sure?'

Olivia almost nodded instinctively, but then she paused. Only a few days previously she had told her maths teacher that she hadn't been able to do her homework because she had been ill. In truth she'd simply forgotten to do it. Or when her grandmother asked her to come to church with her, she usually made up an excuse as well.

'But whenever I lie, it's only a tiny bit,' she tried to justify herself.

'So you think a little lie isn't a lie?'

Olivia sank deeper and deeper into the rocking chair. She had manoeuvred herself into a dead end and knew there was no escaping this situation. Sheepishly, she shook her head.

'It only happens very rarely though.'

The old woman gave her a sympathetic smile.

'Don't worry, you're not the only one. I'd even say that it's almost impossible to find a person who never lies. It seems to be one of humanity's greatest passions and they just don't want to let go of it.'

Silence on both sides.

'So?'

'So what?'

'What about you? Why do you lie?'

Olivia slowly breathed in and out and thought of the two examples that had crossed her mind. The homework she hadn't done and her excuses to get out of going to church.

'I either lie because I don't want to get into trouble, or because I don't want to hurt the other person.'

'Which brings us back to fear again,' Miss God said. 'Because in reality you are scared of getting into trouble, aren't you?'

Olivia considered this for a moment. Yes, it was probably some kind of fear. Not terribly dreadful but certainly an uncomfortable sensation. It was a confrontation she rather wanted to avoid.

'Okay, so maybe I'm scared,' she finally said, 'and that's why I lie. But I don't know where this fear comes from.'

'Where do all other feelings come from?'

'From my heart?'

The old woman smiled.

'Yes, from your heart! And it's the same with fear: it has to do with something deep inside of you. So, it's not so much about the potential trouble you might get into but the fear of admitting to a mistake. Because if you hadn't made a mistake, there wouldn't be a reason to get into trouble.'

'And why should I be scared of admitting mistakes?'

'Because mistakes are hard on your infallible ego.'

'My ego?'

'Yes. The voice inside of you that tries to convince you that you are better than others and that you always do everything right.'

'And where does this voice come from? Also from my heart?'

'No,' Miss God smiled, 'it comes from your head! They're just confused thoughts that develop during life. Everyone has them. They try to tell you that any criticism of you is unjustified and that you can only survive and find happiness if you're the best. But obviously that's nonsense! First, because survival and happiness don't require you to defeat others, and second, because it's impossible to not make any mistakes.'

Olivia found the whole ego thing a bit too complicated.

'And what's with the other reason? If I lie because I don't want to hurt someone? If my grandmother would like me to go to church with her, but I don't feel like it and tell her that I have to study for school.'

'That too has to do with the desire to do everything right. You're scared of disappointing your grandmother, because if you disappoint her it means you're no longer the perfect granddaughter.'

'But my grandmother doesn't expect me to do everything perfectly.'

'Of course not. But you still fear that you might disappoint her because your irrational thoughts make you insecure. So just to be safe, you choose to hide behind a lie.' She thought for a moment. 'What if your grandmother found out you've lied to her? Put yourself into her situation and imagine how you would feel if you discovered that someone hasn't told you the truth.'

Olivia's eyes wandered towards the sea; she felt slightly ashamed. No, it wasn't a nice feeling to be lied to. As a child she knew about this all too well, because the truth was often hidden from children. She remembered the day she was told that her uncle was ill. He's just got a cold, no need to worry, they had said. But by this time the cancer had already attacked his lungs and the doctors had given him only a few months to live. Her parents had only told her what was really going on when death was already waiting around the corner. She had been furious and couldn't understand why they had kept her in the dark for so long.

'One day, most lies come to the surface anyway,' the old woman said. 'So really it's futile to try and hide the truth.'

A strong gust of wind swept across the veranda, silencing them both for a few moments.

'And yet everybody lies,' Olivia said when the wind had calmed down.

'Indeed. People lie and cheat to avoid inconvenient facts or to gain some benefit. Children, parents, friends, teachers, priests and presidents, all happily partake in it. It's a bit like stealing, a real national sport! And in the end, who is there left to believe?' The old woman sighed and leaned against the wall of the hut. 'Apart from me, of course.'

'Of course,' Olivia replied with a smile. 'After all, why should God lie?'

They grinned at each other. Olivia turned to the side to see where her dog was. Albert was still lying on the carpet snoring peacefully. He was probably the only one she could really trust, Olivia thought. The only one who was always honest with her.

'And teachers lie as well?' she dug deeper.

'Well, not with bad intentions. But for example, when they say that you can only find a decent job if you have good grades, it simply doesn't correspond with reality. Because there are many successful people who got bad grades at school, just like there are many people who were really good at school but aren't successful in their job. So the teachers unnecessarily scare students into believing something that isn't true.'

Olivia nodded vigorously. Grades, what an annoying invention!

'They also present some things as absolute truths, even though many different views exist,' the old woman continued. 'They might not tell lies, but they often act as if a few puzzle pieces were enough to see the whole picture. It happens in history class, in religious education and in the natural sciences too. Many teachers and professors talk as if they already know everything, but they still have to learn most things themselves.' She reached for one of her white curls and slowly pulled it to its full length. 'There's really a lot you humans haven't understood yet.'

Olivia nodded. She thought it was more than fair that adults continue to learn as well.

'And then there's television, newspapers and the new media. All these are full of one-sided stories too. Many opinions are offered, but very little truth.'

Olivia rubbed her nose thoughtfully.

'So how do I know what's really true?'

'Difficult indeed. You can only ever be really sure if you've experienced it yourself. If you've fallen out of a tree before, nobody is going to make you believe gravity doesn't exist. Or if you have friends from different countries or who belong to different religions, you already know that countries and religions aren't important when it comes to deciding whether a person is nice or not.'

'And what if I haven't experienced something myself? Who can I believe then?'

Now it was Miss God who had to think for a moment.

'There are people who are close to you and whom you trust more because you know them better. However, this familiarity doesn't mean that you can believe everything they say.' She hesitated. 'I think the best people to trust are the ones who have dealt intensely with a certain subject or question. Those who have done a lot of research and philosophizing and have pursued the root of the problem. Clever minds who want nothing but to find the truth.'

'So how do I recognize such people?'

———————

'So how do I know what's really true?'

'Difficult indeed. You can only ever be really sure if you've experienced it yourself. If you've fallen out of a tree before, nobody is going to make you believe gravity doesn't exist.'

———————

'That's easy,' the old woman said. 'By the curious look in their eyes! Because those who are really interested in the truth, never stop looking for it.'

Olivia immediately thought of her biology teacher. He had that look. His eyes always sparkled with great passion and he was happy every time he didn't know an answer and there was something new for him to discover.

'When it comes to truth, there's one thing which is very important,' Miss God continued after a short pause. 'Something that you already practise wonderfully.'

Olivia's curiosity had been sparked.

'What is it?'

'Asking questions! Because questions keep the search for truth alive.'

They both smiled.

'A life without questions isn't really healthy either,' the old woman added. 'Because whether you're a student or a professor, if you believe that you already know everything, your thinking is highly limited. You're not open to new possibilities and new knowledge, you're not surprised, you're not amazed and you're not investigating. How is anyone supposed to evolve like that?'

Olivia imagined what it would be like if Miss God were her teacher at school. She probably wouldn't have to learn so many useless things and everything would be much more fun. Instead of stuffing her brain with outdated facts, Miss God would encourage her to embark on an exciting expedition.

She glanced at the sky. The sun had gone down quite a bit since she last looked. It was probably time for her to leave.

'So what shall we do with number eight?'

'We could do the same as with the theft commandment,' the old woman replied. 'That is, using the opposite. So instead of "You shall not lie" we could say "You shall be honest". Or more directly, "Be honest".'

'Yes, that would be the easiest,' Olivia said.

'Or even better, "Be honest with yourself"! Because after all that's the first step, not to lie to yourself. To be authentic and not try to fool yourself. To always strive for the truth and to be aware, despite the tempting voice of your ego, that you may also be wrong.'

Olivia was about to agree with a nod, but then she hesitated. Deep inside she felt a growing resistance against a total cheating ban. Yes, it's important to be honest, but always? In every situation? She moved her mouth from side to side expressing her doubt.

'What about blabbermouths?' she suddenly asked. 'Honesty may be important, but to me getting ratted out feels a lot worse than lies.'

'Yes, you're right. There are also cases where you lie out of necessity, to protect yourself or someone else. In a situation like that it might not be appropriate to be totally honest.'

Silence.

'Do you have any other ideas?'

'How about: "Stay curious"?' Olivia suggested.

'"Stay curious",' Miss God repeated in a soft voice. 'I like that. Because if people always stay curious about the world and about themselves, they'll automatically move closer to the truth.'

She rummaged for the pen and notepad, and wrote the two words down. Then she turned to her visitor again.

'If we face the truth and are completely honest, humans will probably never stop lying, denying and deceiving. At least not until they tame their egos. And that may still take quite some time …'

9
Love

livia rose from her rocking chair with a heavy heart.

'I really have to go now.'

'That's a shame,' Miss God said, slightly disappointed, 'we've almost gone through all the commandments. But you've really helped me so far. Thank you for that!'

'You're welcome,' Olivia replied. 'Could I use your toilet before I go?'

'Sure. When you go inside, it's the door on the far left. You can't miss it.'

Olivia entered the hut and let her eyes wander through the room to orientate herself. Curious as she was, she naturally seized the opportunity to see how God lives.

To the right of the entrance was a kitchenette, just off the wall, and behind it she saw a small table and two folding chairs. On the other side of the room was a large bed and next to it a small shelf unit holding a lamp and a few books. There was also a wardrobe against the back wall, that was all. Well, there wasn't actually space for much else anyway. Everything was tidy and reduced to the essentials. A simple home, without any luxuries, but friendly and inviting.

She opened the bathroom door next to the wardrobe, went inside, closed the door and sat down on the toilet. It was indeed a shame, she thought, that this unexpected encounter had already come to an end. If anyone had told her that she would spend the afternoon with an old woman who claimed to be God as little as a few hours ago, she wouldn't have considered it possible. And yes, the whole situation still seemed a bit strange to her, but nevertheless she was glad she had stayed this long.

Suddenly a loud roar of thunder pulled her out of her thoughts. The whole hut began to shake and creak and it seemed as if everything would collapse at any moment. Olivia jumped up and ran outside.

'What happened?' she asked frightened, as she reached the veranda.

'Just a storm,' the old woman said, while remaining peacefully seated on her bench.

Growling thunder sounded once more, then a few flashes of lightning. Albert came whimpering to Olivia and hid behind her legs. He was always terrified by the loud bangs.

'Where did that suddenly come from? The sun was shining only a moment ago.'

Miss God shrugged her shoulders.

'An autumn storm like this can develop quickly, especially here on the coast.'

Then it started to rain.

'Perhaps you had better wait for a bit,' the old woman said calmly. 'I'm sure it won't last long.'

Olivia took two steps to the edge of the veranda and saw a big black wall of rain coming swiftly towards her. Exactly from the direction in which she had to return.

'Are you sure that it won't last long?'

'Yes, it's only a passing storm. In twenty minutes it will probably all be over.'

Alright, Olivia thought. It didn't make any sense to get completely soaked over twenty minutes. Besides, it wasn't a very good idea to walk along the beach when there was lightning around. Her mother and father would probably worry, after all they didn't know she was in a sheltered place. But there was nothing she could do about it now. And in a way being able to postpone the return to her parents a little longer worked out in her favour.

The storm got stronger and stronger and blew some rain on to the veranda, which meant the rocking chair wasn't a dry option any more. She joined the old woman on the bench and leaned her back against the wall. Albert crawled under her and hid his eyes behind his paws.

By now, the initial drops had turned into wild streams. Olivia had never experienced such a torrential downpour, it seemed like the whole sea was falling from the sky! The rain rattled on the roof incessantly and with full force, making so much noise that any kind of conversation was temporarily impossible.

They sat there in silence, watching the fascinating natural spectacle. The clouds and the wind had increased during the last hours, yet it still felt as if the storm had appeared out of nowhere. Olivia stopped short – what if God had summoned the storm? And not just any God, but Miss God! It was a crazy thought, but could such a downpour really be a coincidence, just when she wanted to leave? Suppose the old woman really was God, and suppose God couldn't rule over people but could control the weather – wouldn't it be possible then that Miss God had done something so that she could discuss the last two commandments with her?

A cold shiver ran down Olivia's spine. Carefully she squinted to the side, trying to catch a glimpse of the old woman's face. Miss God was sitting quietly next to her, watching the storm with great admiration. More lightning fired from the black wall and another powerful thunder roar made poor Albert tremble. Olivia caressed him, then let her eyes wander back to the storm as well.

How could she find out whether her thoughts were crazy or not? How could she expose Miss God as a liar and win the game? So far, the old woman had either provided a good answer to all her questions or she had skilfully sidestepped them. Once again, Olivia rubbed her nose thoughtfully. Was she really sitting here with the almighty creator? Or had she perhaps lost her mind long before, given that she even considered such a possibility? Or maybe she had simply immersed herself into her role too deeply? She kept pondering. If only she knew where this mysterious woman had come from.

The spectacle continued for a few minutes, then the rain lessened a bit and the deafening rattling on the roof ceased.

'How did you actually become God?'

The old woman was surprised by the question.

'How am I supposed to know? You can't ask a fish how he became a fish.'

Olivia rolled her eyes and shook her head at the same time. It was hopeless.

'And where were you before you created the world?' she tried nonetheless.

Miss God leaned forward and stared at the sky as if she were looking for something.

'You can't see it right now but the star on which I used to live is all the way over there, near the sun,' she said matter-of-factly. 'But eventually I got bored. There were only tiny bacteria, no humans, no animals, not even trees. That's why I created Earth.'

'And where were you born? You must be from somewhere, no?'

The old woman smiled.

'As far as I know, I've always existed.'

'Always?'

'Yes. Remember, I am life.'

'But life must have begun at some point too.'

Miss God shook her head.

'Do you remember when we talked about death earlier on? I told you that death is a part of life. That, in reality, there is no beginning and no end.'

Olivia nodded.

'And if life has no beginning and no end, it means that it has always existed and that it always will.' She paused for a moment and looked deeply into the eyes of her visitor. 'Life is constantly changing but it was never born and will never die. It exists always and everywhere. Just like you and me, here and now.'

Another roll of thunder echoed through the air. There were still black clouds above them and it hadn't stopped raining either, but beyond the clouds they could already see the blue sky again. Just like the old woman had predicted.

'Shall we continue with the commandments while you're waiting?'

What if God had summoned the storm? And not just any God, but Miss God! It was a crazy thought, but could such a downpour really be a coincidence, just when she wanted to leave? Suppose the old woman really was God, and suppose God couldn't rule over people but could control the weather.

'Alright,' Olivia agreed, although she couldn't shake the feeling that Miss God had manipulated the situation. Such a sudden storm, that really wasn't normal.

'Wonderful!' Miss God said. 'Number nine: "Thou shalt not covet your neighbour's wife".'

'Great,' the girl sighed.

'What?'

'They're using the strange language again. And besides, it sounds like someone owns the woman.'

'I'm afraid that's exactly how it's meant. Men owned women by law in those days.'

'Really? So, like a dog, or a sheep?'

'Yes, something like that.'

The rain picked up again, forcing another break in the conversation. Olivia didn't want to imagine what it would be like to be owned by a man. How horrible to be someone's servant your whole life! Fortunately, this time the rattling noise only lasted for a few seconds and so her thoughts of a servant's existence moved on as quickly as the downpour.

'What's the difference between the ninth and the sixth commandment?' she asked.

'The sixth commandment is originally about divorce, whereas the ninth is about a common reason for divorce – lacking faithfulness.' The old woman hesitated for a moment. 'Do you know what faithfulness means?'

Olivia looked up, offended.

'I'm eleven, not three!' she said indignantly.

'I'm sorry,' Miss God replied immediately. 'I didn't mean it like that. Of course you know what faithfulness means. The problem is, sadly, many others do not.'

This time Olivia nodded in agreement. Once, her parents had had a problem with faithfulness too. Luckily, she herself hadn't had such an experience yet, but she imagined it to be similar to the truth: telling a lie yourself can be fun, but it never feels good if others lie to you.

'But what about people who aren't married? To them faithfulness is meaningless.'

'That's true. If you're not in a relationship, you can't be unfaithful.' Miss God took a quick look at her notes. 'Besides, faithfulness is already covered by the new sixth commandment now. Because if two people keep their word after they've agreed to be faithful, there won't be any problems.'

Another roll of thunder. A bit softer than before but still loud enough to frighten the little terrier. The old woman reached under the bench and gently laid her hand on his head. He calmed down immediately.

'Perhaps we can use faithfulness anyway,' she said after a while. 'Instead of being faithful to another person you could be faithful to your own heart.'

'But how can I be unfaithful to my heart?' Olivia wondered.

Miss God smiled. Then she pointed to her head.

'By thinking too much.'

'You don't want me to think?'

'No,' the old woman laughed, 'I didn't say that. Thinking is important, but not every life question can be answered by logic, reason and science alone. At least, not if you want to be happy.'

Olivia looked puzzled.

'Let me give you an example. Imagine you were a few years older and you're contemplating which profession you should learn. After much back and forth you end up with two options, to either become a teacher or a musician. Your mind tells you that teaching is a better career because it offers you a lot of security; your heart beats for the music though. Both are attractive possibilities, but only one will make you really happy.' She hesitated for a moment. 'If you didn't trust your heart, you'd never find the courage to at least give the music a try.'

Olivia knew what she meant. However, for this decision she wouldn't need reason nor heart. Her? A teacher? Dear God, no!

'You know,' the old woman said, 'an able mind can help people with a lot of things. It can protect them and nourish them, it can solve thousands of problems and even carry them far into the universe.' A final roar of thunder was heard in the distance. 'But only the heart can lead people to love.'

Olivia felt an excited tingling in her belly. Love, truth and a happy life, suddenly it all fell into place.

'And where love is, that's also where true happiness is, right?'

'Exactly!'

Miss God put her arm around the girl like a proud grandmother and smiled at her.

'Where love is, that's where true happiness is,' she repeated. 'Now we just have to translate it into a good phrase for the commandments.'

'I already had something earlier on, wait!'

Olivia squinted her eyes and pondered.

'Faithfulness ... love ... heart ... trust.' She squinted a little harder, then it burst out of her. 'I've got it! "Trust your heart"!'

Miss God smiled even more now.

And her heart danced.

Love

10
Gratitude

he thunder had passed. Albert crawled cautiously out of his hiding place under the bench and sniffed the wonderfully fresh air the storm had left behind. It was still raining a little, but judging by the sky this would end in five or ten minutes as well. Miss God didn't have much time left to discuss the last commandment before Olivia would have to leave.

'There's one left. Do you think we can do it?'

'Yes, we can do it.'

'Great!' the old woman cheered. 'So, here's number ten: "Thou shalt not covet your neighbour's property".' And before her young guest could say anything, she added: 'I know, that strange language again. Just ignore it.'

Olivia nodded.

'It sounds similar to the seventh commandment. The one about stealing.'

'A little bit, yes. But just as unfaithfulness is a reason for divorce, coveting is a reason for stealing. It's much more about the actual cause of the problem because without coveting, that is, without having the desire, you wouldn't develop the urge to steal something from someone.'

'And where does the desire come from?'

Both let their eyes wander straight ahead and stare into nothingness.

In the meantime, Albert had ventured to the edge of the veranda and was happily snatching up raindrops with his long tongue.

'I think it has to do with a feeling of emptiness,' Miss God finally said. 'People always think something is lacking. No matter how much or how little they possess, there's always something they don't have yet. And as long as they don't have it, their desire won't let them rest. Like hungry animals, they want to get this thing that is missing to complete their happiness. But they overlook the fact that it's their desires and wishes that create the inner emptiness in the first place.'

A short silence.

'Does this mean I shouldn't have any wishes?'

The old woman smiled compassionately.

'If you really want to be happy, wishes aren't very helpful, no. However, it also depends on how much you let yourself be influenced by them. Every now and then a few wishes aren't really a problem, but if they start to control your life you run the risk of losing your freedom.'

Olivia thought of the bicycle she had really wanted a few years ago. Out of sheer desperation she had barely been able to sleep, convinced she was doomed to eternal sadness without a bike. She had been willing to do anything for it! So when her parents had asked her if she would celebrate the communion, she hadn't had to think twice. And, true, the first weeks with the desired bicycle had been great, she had been over the moon and spent every spare minute with her new treasure. But soon afterwards, the initial excitement had waned and a new wish had taken its place. In retrospect she wondered whether all the hours with the annoying priest had been too high a price to pay. Sure, she had also made her grandmother happy, which was a nice side effect, but still a bitter aftertaste remained. So much wasted time, all for a bicycle.

'Even in Moses' time, desire created a great many problems,' Miss God began. 'That's why I talked to him about it. People were envious when their neighbour had more cattle or owned a bigger house, and that caused a lot of dissatisfaction amongst everyone.' She paused for a moment. 'Unfortunately, that hasn't improved to this day. On the contrary, envy is still widely spread and on top of that greed has increased a lot too. In the past there were also greedy people, especially kings and Pharaohs, but nowhere near as many. Today it has reached such proportions that almost every other person seems to be affected by materialism. Food, clothing, furniture, photos and even holidays – it always has to be more and more of everything.'

Olivia immediately thought of her cousin, her aunt and her aunt's permanently ill-humoured husband. They were by far the worst.

The first weeks with the desired bicycle had been great, she had been over the moon and spent every spare minute with her new treasure. But soon afterwards, the initial excitement had waned and a new wish had taken its place.

'I know a family who spends every Saturday from early in the morning till late at night in the shopping centre. They buy so much they have to move every few years because all the new stuff doesn't fit into their flat anymore.'

The old woman sighed.

'It's terrible, isn't it? It has got totally out of hand. Always buying and adding more things, is that supposed to be the meaning of life?'

Another sigh.

'I would go as far as to say that greed has become my biggest competitor. If there were other divine beings, I wouldn't be afraid of them, but I fear the material gods a lot. Slowly but surely, they are taking my place. They are worshipped, considered sacred and hardly anyone doubts them.'

Miss God let her shoulders slump with disappointment.

'Of course, there are many nice things you can buy, things that are useful and fun, but it's just sad that people become so dependent on these material gods.'

Olivia stared at her thoughtfully. Once again she had got stuck on something else.

'Why am I actually here?' she wanted to know.

Miss God shot her a questioning look.

'You just talked about the meaning of life. So, why am I here, on Earth, in this body? Why all this?'

'But I've already told you. I was bored so I created the humans. You are here to entertain me,' she winked at her.

'Come on, just tell me!' Olivia replied. 'I really want to know.'

'Why do you think you're here?'

Always these counter questions, Olivia thought. Why couldn't she just get a straight answer?

'I don't know.'

'No idea?' the old woman asked.

'No.'

Olivia remained stubborn. Even if she had known an answer, this time she would have kept silent. But she really didn't have a clue why humans and the Earth existed. What could be the meaning of life?

'Some people believe that everything is just chance and randomness,' Miss God said after a little pause. 'Others are convinced that they have some kind of mission in this world. To fight for the survival of humankind, or to help others. And then there are also people who think that the purpose of life is all about fun and pleasure.'

She hesitated for a second.

'Actually, they're all right. In a way everything is a coincidence, but in this coincidence every person plays a crucial role. Everyone is responsible for life, everyone has the opportunity to make the world a little bit better. And of course, life should also be fun! A friend of mine once said that every minute without a smile is a wasted minute. I totally agree with him.'

'And what about fate? Does it exist?'

'You mean is everything pre-determined?'

'Yes.'

The old woman thought for a moment.

'Some things are indeed pre-programmed. Starting at birth, it's like you swim in a river and if you let yourself drift, your life is already set. What is often forgotten though is the fact that you can swim to the shore and continue by foot at any time. After all, many routes lead to the sea.'

At least that's something, Olivia thought. She had never liked the idea of being helplessly at fate's mercy. However, she still hadn't received a proper answer to her original question yet.

'But what's your own opinion?' she tried again. 'Why are we here?'

'Well, I am here because ...'

'I know, you are here because you've always been here,' Olivia interrupted her. 'But what about me and all the other people?'

Miss God looked at her seriously for a moment. Then she smiled.

'Alright then. Personally, I think that you are here to learn.'

Olivia grimaced. The idea didn't exactly make her jump for joy.

'And what am I supposed to learn?'

'The art of living.'

'The art of living?'

'Yes. How can you use your available time in the best possible way? What's important and what's not? How can you spread love and find happiness? Unfortunately, all those things aren't taught at school. Hence you have to acquire this knowledge yourself.'

'And how do I start with that?'

'You already have,' the old woman laughed. 'You are right in the middle of it! Or why do you think you've been sitting here with me?'

'But ...' Olivia began, then the words failed her. Was that the reason she had met God? To learn?

'So basically, you invited me here for a class?'

Another laugh.

'Yes, that's one way of looking at it. And you know which your most important lesson was today?'

Olivia thought about it, but she wasn't sure.

'Who is your real teacher?' Miss God helped her.

'You?'

'That's right. And who am I?'

Now Olivia remembered.

'Life.'

'Yes! So, it's not God who is your teacher, but life.'

They both smiled. She could get used to this idea, Olivia thought, having life as her teacher.

'If I were you, I wouldn't worry too much about whether there's a deeper meaning for your existence or not,' the old woman continued. 'The only thing that matters is that we're alive, right now, in this moment. That we can have a great conversation, that we breathe fresh air and hear the beautiful sound of the sea.' She gazed thoughtfully at the horizon. 'There are so many people who are waiting for a saviour. But I wonder what they want to be saved from? From life? After all, this moment is all we have. And it's also everything we need.'

The last raindrops fell to the ground and shortly afterwards the sun came through the clouds again. In about an hour it would set in heavenly colours.

'I really have to go back now,' Olivia said, knowing that, without the storm, she had no excuse to stay any longer.

Albert immediately started wagging his tail in anticipation. He sensed they'd be on the move soon and he'd be able to whizz up and down the beach again.

'Alright,' Miss God replied and rose up from the bench. 'I will accompany you to the dune, so we can finish the tenth commandment along the way.'

Olivia got up as well and signalled Albert with a nod that he was free to go. The little terrier didn't have to be told twice – he jumped forward and ran off, happily barking. The other two crossed the veranda and walked towards the beach together.

'I just had an idea,' the old woman said. 'If the emptiness inside a person is the cause of desire, then the question would be how this emptiness is created in the first place. Why do people never get enough, why are they never completely satisfied? Perhaps it's like a bucket with a hole. No matter how much water you add, the bucket never fills up. So the solution is ...'

'... to fix the hole.'

'Yes. And do you know how we can fix the hole?'

Olivia shrugged her shoulders.

'With gratitude! Because if you feel grateful, the emptiness is filled with happiness. If you appreciate the things you already have – a favourite dress, friends, sunsets – then there is no room left for greed and all those yearning desires that are stealing your peace.'

Life really is full of countless gifts, Olivia thought. Especially if all the gifts we take for granted are considered too. A tasty pizza, a warm shower or simply a blooming flower – things that seem like a given at first, but if you look closely they are all little miracles.

'And the most precious gift you've already received anyway,' the old woman said, as if she had read the girl's thoughts. 'It's your heartbeat! The pulse that connects you to everything. If you are aware of this and if you love this wonderful life, what should be lacking?'

Olivia knew what she meant, even though the part about the heartbeat sounded a bit weird.

'So let's call the tenth commandment: "Be grateful",' she suggested.

They had reached the highest point of the dune. Miss God stopped and smiled.

'Be grateful. Yes, that's the perfect ending!'

With bright eyes she turned to Olivia, opened her arms and gave her a long hug.

'It's been nice talking with you.'

'Yes, it has,' Olivia agreed. 'Thank you for the hot chocolate and the biscuits.'

'Thank you for your help and your time. And for your trust!'

Olivia nodded contentedly.

'I've really enjoyed your game,' she added.

Miss God gave her a puzzled look.

'Which game?'

Silence.

Then she winked at her one last time and let her eyes wander to the sea.

'Just look at those waves! Slowly rolling to the shore, steadily and not too high for me. Perfect conditions for another round of surfing.'

They smiled.

'Take care,' the old woman said.

'You too.'

Olivia turned around, called Albert and left Miss God alone on the sand dune.

Soon she was strolling over the soft sand along the beach again, almost as if nothing had happened. She shook her head, laughing – who was going to believe this story?

Gratitude

Epilogue

hen Olivia returned to her parents, she was hit with the next storm. As expected, they had been really worried and had almost called the police. Where the hell had she been, they wanted to know. But on her way back Olivia had already decided she wouldn't tell them about her encounter with Miss God. They wouldn't believe her anyway and she'd probably get into even more trouble. So instead she said that the storm had surprised her and that she had found shelter on the terrace of an empty beach bar. It didn't help though – she was grounded for a whole week because she had acted irresponsibly and should have returned much earlier.

Half an hour later they were driving along the coastal road, leaving the small town. Olivia sat on the back seat in silence while her parents argued about whether they should punish her further by taking away her mobile phone. They never missed an opportunity to complicate each other's lives.

Olivia gazed through the window and thought about her conversation with the old woman. She had enjoyed talking and listening to her, and contemplating the questions of life. Whether the ten new commandments would change the world, she didn't know, but in her own little cosmos they had already created a little more confidence. She felt the new words were much more encouraging, more powerful and also more realistic. And perhaps most importantly, the new commandments didn't mention God a single time! This way they'd work for everyone and not only for the followers of a certain religion; they would connect people rather than divide them into competing groups. Actually, separating faith from religion was one of the most valuable things Olivia had taken from the conversation. Because she did want to believe in something, just without the pressure and constraint of having to follow the ideas of others.

They had almost reached the end of the narrow coastal road, and the car slowed to turn right on to a bigger country lane. Olivia looked at the horizon and watched the red, shimmering sun sink elegantly into the sea. Only one question remained, she thought. Had it been a game or not?

Exactly at that moment she spotted a lone surfer in the distance, riding a long wave across the deep-blue water. Olivia started – it had to be very close to the old woman's hut.

'No, that's not possible,' she said to herself. It couldn't actually be ... or could it? What if it really were Miss God surfing the last wave before sundown?

The car turned right and Olivia threw herself around, trying to hold on to the moment a little longer. She stared through the rear window mesmerized, until wave, surfer and sun had disappeared. And then she suddenly realized how she could answer her question: of course she knew it had been only a game – but nevertheless she decided to believe something else.

Olivia had to wait four months before she returned to the small coastal town. It was the first week of the new year and her parents wanted to recover from the Christmas stress for a few days. As usual that didn't work out as planned because they wasted all their energy on constant quarrels. Fortunately, Olivia's little terrier was happy to escape the never-ending drama with her. And besides, there was someone she really wanted to visit.

Since her return she had often thought about that special afternoon with Miss God. She had dreamed of her for many nights; she had seen the old woman sitting in front of her on the bench again and had felt her loving smile. She missed her, like one misses a good friend. However, the doubts had grown as well – had the encounter really happened or did Miss God live only as a ghost in her head? She didn't have any evidence of her existence – no witnesses, no photos, not even a telephone number. She wanted to keep believing in her, but it was getting more and more difficult.

'No, that's not possible', she said to herself. It couldn't actually be ... or could it? What if it really were Miss God surfing the last wave before sundown?

The morning after she had arrived with her parents, Olivia used her parents' first fight as an opportunity to run off with Albert.

An unpleasant, icy wind was blowing along the beach, so no one else had dared to set foot outside. But Olivia didn't mind the cold because she had a clear goal in mind: she hurriedly walked along the shore, eager to reach the hut and to banish her doubts once and for all.

When she crossed the dune full of hope a little while later, she saw Miss God's modest home and suddenly felt her heart drop. Something was wrong.

She continued until she was standing directly in front of the hut. Everything seemed deserted. The shutters were down, the door locked and the veranda covered in a thick layer of sand. Far and wide, there was no sign that anyone had lived here recently.

Disappointed, Olivia felt her shoulders slump. She had really been looking forward to seeing the old woman again, had visualized the moment of their second encounter over and over again. And now? Now it felt as if she had imagined it all. She didn't want to accept it and desperately searched for a sign that would bring Miss God back to life. But walking around the property she was presented with the same evidence: no open window, no footprints and no surfboard either. Nothing.

When she got back to the front she stopped for a moment and sadly regarded the empty hut. She sighed and was just about to turn around and walk back when she saw Albert lying under the bench, wagging his tail excitedly. He seemed to be sniffing at something. Olivia felt her pulse quicken. She rushed over to him, knelt and began digging under the bench. It didn't take long until her fingers hit a flat, loose piece of wood. Hastily she pulled it out, stood up and shook off the remaining sand.

Her whole face gleamed with joy and happiness. It was the sign she had hoped for! A solid proof that the wonderful encounter with Miss God hadn't been a dream. She held the wooden board in front of her and calmly read the engraved words ...

1 Love life
2 Respect others
3 Make time for yourself
4 Honour nature
5 Forgive
6 Keep your word
7 Share
8 Stay curious
9 Trust your heart
10 Be grateful

This edition published 2020
by Ammonite Press
an imprint of Guild of Master Craftsman Publications Ltd
Castle Place, 166 High Street, Lewes,
East Sussex, BN7 1XU, United Kingdom
www.ammonitepress.com

Text © Claus Mikosch, 2020
Illustrations © Kate Chesterton, 2020
Copyright in the Work © GMC Publications Ltd, 2020

ISBN 978 1 78145 390 2

A catalogue record for this book is available from the British Library.

Publisher: Jason Hook
Design Manager: Robin Shields
Editor: Jane Roe

Colour reproduction by GMC Reprographics
Printed and bound in China

How was
the book?
Please
post your
feedback:
#MissGod

AMMONITE
PRESS

www.ammonitepress.com

FSC
www.fsc.org

MIX

Paper from
responsible sources

FSC® C016973